Obedience to Christ
Striving for The Greatest Wisdom of All

A. W. Tozer
& Caleb Sinclair

GRAPEVINE INDIA

Published by

GRAPEVINE INDIA PUBLISHERS PVT LTD

www.grapevineindia.com
Delhi | Mumbai
email: grapevineindiapublishers@gmail.com

Ordering Information:
Quantity sales: Special discounts are available on quantity
purchases by corporations, associations, and others.
For details, reach out to the publisher.

First published by Grapevine India 2022

Introduction

The word Christian is everywhere now. A simple global statistic gives us an estimate of how many people claim to be following Christ. Following Christ is, of course, what the term Christian means.

One would expect that a world with such a large percentage of Christ-followers would be fundamentally different from how it is today. All who call themselves Christian have not truly understood what it means to be Christian. I say this not to condemn or to judge. It's just that the term has been thrown and tossed about so much that its true meaning has been lost.

Tozer underlines the teaching of the Bible—obedience is evidence of salvation. Self-assured self-titling is no means proof of the truth. Conviction and faith do have their place in a Christian's life, but they must be founded on biblical authority. And the Bible equates Christian with obedient. If you say you love God, it will be evident in your life.

Precious blood has been shed for the forgiveness of our sins.

For Tozer, there is no mincing of words when it comes to preaching biblical truth. The life of obedience is not meant to be an easy one, but it is the wisest course of life. It takes into account the purpose for which man was made, the immensity of the gift which has been given him, and his eternal and glorious future. And he makes his choice to live a life that is not wasteful.

I can only pray that you, dear reader, will make that choice too.

– Caleb Sinclair

1.The Freedom to Disobey

God's sovereignty is the attribute by which He rules His entire creation, and to be sovereign, God must be all-knowing, all-powerful, and absolutely free. The sovereignty of God is a fact well established in the Scriptures and declared aloud by the logic of truth. But admittedly it raises certain problems which have not to this time been satisfactorily solved.

One of the real problems created by the doctrine of the divine sovereignty has to do with the will of man. If God rules His universe by His sovereign decrees, how is it possible for man to exercise free choice? And if he cannot exercise freedom of choice, how can he be held responsible for his conduct? Is he not a mere puppet whose actions are determined by a behind-the-scenes God who pulls the strings as it pleases Him?

The attempt to answer these questions has divided the Christian church neatly into two camps which have borne the names of two distinguished theologians, Jacobus Arminius and John Calvin. Most Christians are content to get into one camp or the other and deny either sovereignty to God or free will to man. It appears possible, however, to reconcile these two positions without doing violence to either, although the effort that follows may prove deficient to partisans of one camp or the other.

Here is my view: God sovereignly decreed that man should be free to exercise moral choice, and man from the beginning has fulfilled that decree by making his choice between good and evil. When he chooses to do evil, he does not thereby countervail counteract the sovereign will of God but fulfills it, inasmuch as the eternal decree decided not which choice the man should make but that he should be free to make it. If in His absolute freedom God has willed to give man limited freedom, who is there to stay His hand or say, "What doest thou?"

Man's will is free because God is sovereign. A God less than sovereign could not bestow moral freedom upon His creatures. He would be afraid to do so.

An Illustration

Perhaps a homely illustration might help us to understand. An ocean liner leaves New York bound for Liverpool. Its destination has been determined by proper authorities. Nothing can change it. This is at least a faint picture of sovereignty.

On board the liner are several scores of passengers. These are not in chains, neither are their activities determined for them by decree. They are completely free to move about as they will. They eat, sleep, play, lounge about on the deck, read, talk, altogether as they please; but all the while the great liner is carrying them steadily onward toward a predetermined port.

Both freedom and sovereignty are present here and they do not contradict each other. So it is, I believe, with man's freedom and the sovereignty of God. The mighty liner of God's sovereign design keeps its steady course over the sea of history. God moves undisturbed and unhindered toward the fulfilment of those eternal purposes which He purposed in Christ Jesus before the world began. We do not know all that is included in those purposes, but enough has been disclosed to furnish us with a broad outline of things to come and to give us good hope and firm assurance of future well-being.

We know that God will fulfil every promise made to the prophets. We know that sinners will some day be cleansed out of the earth. We know that a ransomed company will enter into the joy of God and that the righteous will shine forth in the kingdom of their Father.

We know that God's perfections will yet receive universal acclamation, that all created intelligences will own Jesus Christ Lord to the glory of God the Father, that the present imperfect order will be done away, and a new heaven and a new earth be established forever.

Toward all this God is moving with infinite wisdom and perfect precision of action. No one can dissuade Him from His purposes; nothing can turn Him aside from His plans.

Since He is omniscient, there can be no unforeseen circumstances, no accidents. As He is sovereign, there can be no countermanded orders, no breakdown in authority; and as He is omnipotent, there can be no want of power to achieve His chosen ends. God is sufficient unto Himself for all these things.

In the meanwhile, things are not as smooth as this quick outline might suggest. The mystery of iniquity is already at work. Within the broad field of God's sovereign and permissive will, the deadly conflict of good with evil continues with increasing fury. God will yet have His way in the whirlwind and the storm, but the storm and the whirlwind are here, and as responsible beings we must make our choice in the present moral situation.

Certain things have been decreed by the free determination of God. One of these is the law of choice and consequences. God has decreed that all who willingly commit themselves to His Son Jesus Christ in the obedience of faith shall receive eternal life and become sons of God. He has also decreed that all who love darkness and continue in rebellion against the high authority of heaven shall remain in a state of spiritual alienation and suffer eternal death at last.

Reducing the whole matter to individual terms, we arrive at some vital and highly personal conclusions. In the moral conflict now raging around us, whoever is on God's side is on the winning side and cannot lose; whoever is on the other side is on the losing side and cannot win.

Here there is no chance, no gamble. There is freedom to choose which side we shall be on, but no freedom to negotiate the results of the choice once it is made. By the mercy of God, we may repent a wrong choice and alter the consequences by making a new and right choice. We cannot go beyond that.

The whole matter of moral choice centers around Jesus Christ. Christ stated it plainly: "He that is not with me is against me," and "No man cometh unto the Father, but by me."

The gospel message embodies three distinct elements: an announcement, a command, and a call. It announces the good news of redemption accomplished in mercy; it commands all men everywhere to repent; and it calls all men to surrender to the terms of grace by believing on Jesus Christ as Lord and Savior.

We must all choose whether we will obey the gospel or turn away in unbelief and reject its authority. Our choice is our own, but the consequences of the choice have already been determined by the sovereign will of God, and from this there is no appeal.

Freedom of the Will

It is inherent in the nature of man that his will must be free. Made in the image of God who is completely free, man must enjoy a measure of freedom. This enables him to select his companions for this world and the next. It enables him to yield his soul to whom he will, to give allegiance to God or the devil, to remain a sinner or become a saint.

And God respects this freedom. God once saw everything that He had made, and behold, it was very good. To find fault with the smallest thing God has made is to find fault with its Maker. It is a false humility that would lament that God wrought but imperfectly when He made man in His own image. Sin excepted, there is nothing in human nature to apologize for. This was confirmed forever when the Eternal Son became permanently incarnated in human flesh.

So highly does God regard His handiwork that He will not for any reason violate it. For God to override man's freedom and force him to act contrary to his own will would be to make a mockery of the image of God in man. This God will never do.

Our Lord Jesus looked after the rich young ruler as he walked away, but He did not follow him or attempt to coerce him. The dignity of the young man's humanity forbade that his choices should be made for him by another. To remain a man, he must make his own moral choice.

Christ knew this and permitted him to go his own chosen way. If his human choice took him at last to hell, at least he went there a man. It is better for the moral universe that he should do so, than that he should be jockeyed into a heaven he did not choose, a soulless, will-less automaton.

God will take nine steps toward us, but He will not take the tenth. He will incline us to repent, but He cannot do our repenting for us.

The essence of repentance is that it can only be done by the one who committed the act to be repented of.

God can wait on the sinning man; He can withhold judgment; He can exercise long-suffering to the point where He appears "lax" in His judicial administration; but He cannot force a man to repent. To do this would be to violate the man's freedom and void the gift God originally bestowed upon him.

Where there is no freedom of choice, there can be neither sin nor righteousness, because it is of the nature of both that they be voluntary. However good an act may be, it is not good if it is imposed from without. The act of imposition destroys the moral content of the act and renders it null and void.

For an act to be sinful, the quality of voluntariness must also be present. Sin is the voluntary commission of an act known to be contrary to the will of God. Where there is no moral knowledge or where there is no voluntary choice, the act is not sinful. It cannot be, for sin is the transgression of the law and transgression must be voluntary.

Lucifer became Satan when he made his fateful choice: "*I will ascend above the heights of the clouds; I will be like the most High.*" (Isaiah 14:14)

Clearly here was a choice made against light. Both knowledge and will were present in the act.

Conversely, Christ revealed His holiness when He cried in His agony, "*Not my will, but thine, be done.*" (Luke 22:42)

Here was a deliberate choice made with the full knowledge of the consequences. Here two wills were in temporary conflict—the lower will of the Man who was God, and the higher will of the God who was Man—and the higher will prevailed. Here also was seen in glaring contrast the enormous difference between Christ and Satan; and that difference divides saint from sinner and heaven from hell.

Choosing God's Will

But someone may ask, "When we pray, 'Not my will, but Thine be done,' are we not voiding our will and refusing to exercise the very power of choice which is part of the image of God in us?"

The answer to that question is a flat *No*, but the whole thing deserves further explanation.

No act that is done voluntarily is an abrogation of the freedom of will. If a man chooses the will of God, he is not denying but *exercising* his right of choice. What he is doing is admitting that he is not good enough to desire the highest choice nor is he wise enough to make it, and he is for that reason asking Another who is both wise and good to make his choice for him. And for fallen man this is the ultimate use he should make of his freedom of will.

Tennyson saw this and wrote of Christ,

> *Thou seemest human and divine,*
>
> *The highest, holiest manhood, Thou;*
>
> *Our wills are ours, we know not how;*
>
> *Our wills are ours, to make them Thine.*

There is a lot of sound doctrine in these words—"Our wills are ours, to make them Thine." The secret of saintliness is not the destruction of the will but the submergence of it in the will of God.

The true saint is one who acknowledges that he possesses from God the gift of freedom. He knows that he will never be cudgeled into obedience nor wheedled like a petulant child into doing the will of God; he knows that these methods are unworthy both of God and of his own soul. He knows he is free to make any choice he will, and with that knowledge he chooses forever the blessed will of God.

2.The Foundation of Obedience

Take For Granted

Once Mary and Joseph, with a number of friends and relatives, were travelling back home from Jerusalem and, supposing the young Jesus to be in the company, went a whole day's journey before discovering that He had been left behind.

Their fault was that they took too much for granted. They assumed that what they wanted to believe was what had happened. A simple check at the start of the journey would have saved them a harrowing experience of fear and uncertainty and two days' unnecessary travel.

Theirs was a pardonable fault and one that we ourselves are in great danger of committing. The whole company of evangelicals is travelling home supposing things, some of which may not be true. We had better check before we go any further. Our failure to do so could have more serious consequences than those suffered by Mary and Joseph. It could lead straight to tragedy.

There is danger that we take Christ for granted. We "suppose" that because we hold New Testament beliefs, we are therefore New Testament Christians; but it does not follow. The devil is a better theologian than any of us and is a devil still.

We may, for instance, assume that salvation is possible without repentance. Pardon without penitence is a delusion which simple honesty requires that we expose for what it is. To be forgiven, a sin must be forsaken. This accords with the Scriptures, with common logic and with the experience of the saints of all ages.

We are also in danger of assuming the value of religion without righteousness. Through the various media of public communication, we are being pressured into believing that religion is little more than a beautiful thing capable of bringing courage and peace of mind to a troubled world. Let us resist this effort at brainwashing. The purpose of Christ's redeeming work was to make it possible for bad men to become good—deeply, radically and finally. God translates men out of the kingdom of darkness into the kingdom of the Son of His love. To believe that such translated men must still dwell in darkness is a reflection on the blood of Christ and the wisdom of God.

In spite of all that James said to the contrary, we are still likely to take for granted that faith without works does somehow have a mystic value after all. But "faith worketh by love," said Paul, and where the works of love are absent, we can only conclude that faith is absent also. Faith in faith has displaced faith in God in too many places.

A whole new generation of Christians has come up believing that it is possible to "accept" Christ without forsaking the world. But what saith the Holy Ghost? "*Ye adulterers and adulteresses, know ye not that the friendship of the world is enmity with God? whosoever therefore will be a friend of the world is the enemy of God,*" (James 4:4), and "*If any man love the world, the love of the Father is not in him.*" (1 John 2:15) This requires no comment, only obedience.

We may also erroneously assume that we can experience justification without transformation. Justification and regeneration are not the same; they may be thought apart in theology but they can never be experienced apart in fact. When God declares a man righteous, He instantly sets about to make him righteous. Our error today is that we do not expect a converted man to be a transformed man, and as a result of this error our churches are full of substandard Christians. A revival is, among other things, a return to the belief that real faith invariably produces holiness of heart and righteousness of life.

Without exhausting the list of things wrongly taken for granted I would mention one more: Millions take for granted that it is possible to live for Christ without first having died with Christ. This is a serious error and we dare not leave it unchallenged.

The victorious Christian has known two lives. The first was his life in Adam which was motivated by the carnal mind and can never please God in any way. It can never be converted; it can only die (Romans 8:5-8).

The second life of the Christian is his new life in Christ (Romans 6:11). To live a Christian life with the life of Adam is wholly impossible. Yet multitudes take for granted that it can be done and go on year after year in defeat. And worst of all they accept this half-dead condition as normal.

For our own soul's sake, let us not take too much for granted.

No Two Ways About It

Certain things have been decreed by the free determination of God, and one of these is the law of choice and consequences. God has decreed that all who willingly commit themselves to His Son Jesus Christ in the obedience of faith shall receive eternal life and become sons of God. He has also decreed that all who love darkness and continue in rebellion against the high authority of heaven shall remain in a state of spiritual alienation and suffer eternal death at last.

Do not fail to notice that Jesus could and did say, "I speak and I judge. I speak from the Father." Jesus was not in the business of offering human advice that people could take or leave as they wished. Instead, He always spoke with absolute, final authority. He was not just a man speaking. His was not just advice from a good, religious man. He was God speaking. This, then, was what Jesus told His questioners:

I am from above.... But he that sent me is true; and I speak to the world those things which I have heard of him.... I do nothing of myself; but as my Father hath taught me, I speak these things.... The Father hath not left me alone. (John 8:23, 26, 28–29)

Jesus was declaring that He spoke for the Father, from whose absolute message there was no appeal. This was quite different from what we hear about in ecclesiastical circles today. A bishop says, "It is to be like this...." However, his decree can always be appealed to the archbishop. But when the Lord Jesus Christ speaks, there is no appeal. It is either Jesus or everlasting night. It is either listen to what He says or be forever in ignorance. It is either take His light, or be forever in darkness.

Immediately, someone is bound to protest. "What arrogance! What intolerance! I do not believe Christians should be intolerant!" Well, I can startle such a person a little more. I believe in Christian charity, but I do not believe at all in Christian tolerance.

The person who hates the name of Jesus, who believes that He was not the Son of God but an imposter, deserves charity on our part. I think if I lived next door to such a person, I would not put a fence between us. If I worked with him or her, I would not refuse to be friendly. I believe in Christian charity, but I do not believe in the weak tolerance that we hear preached so often now—the idea that Jesus must tolerate everyone and that the Christian must tolerate every kind of doctrine. I do not believe it for one minute, for there are not a dozen "rights." There is only one "right." There is but one Jesus and one God and one Bible.

When we become so tolerant that we lead people into mental fog and spiritual darkness, we are not acting like Christians. We are acting like cowards! We cannot do better than to remember that when Jesus Christ has spoken, that is it!

When Jesus claimed to have come from the heart of the Father, when He was declared to be the eternal Word who was in the beginning with God, who was and is God, we are hearing truth. Our position is clear. It is not Jesus plus a number of other philosophies. It is Jesus only. He is enough….

An honest person may come to Jesus seeking, yet not understanding. It may take a week or a month, a year or ten years to help him or her understand. But that person can be sure of this: our Lord will never, never say anything but what He has said. Never will He hedge. Never will He put in a footnote, "I didn't quite mean it like that." He said what He meant. He meant what He said. He is the Eternal Word, and we must listen to Him if our discipleship is to be genuine and consistent.

We ought to think with joy about those who are true disciples of Jesus Christ. A true disciple has not taken an impulsive leap in the dark. That person is one who has become a Christian after deep thought and proper consideration. A true disciple has allowed the Word of God to search his or her heart. A true disciple has felt the sense of personal sin and the need to be released from it. A true disciple has come to believe that Jesus Christ is the only person who can release him or her from guilt. A true disciple has committed himself or herself without equivocation, without reservation to Jesus Christ the Savior.

A true disciple does not consider Christianity a part-time commitment. That person has become a Christian in all departments of his or her life. A true disciple has reached the point in Christian experience where there is no turning back. Follow him or her for 24 hours of the day and night. You will find you can count on that person's faithfulness to Christ and his or her joyful abiding in the Word of God.

Long ago I came to the conclusion that if Jesus Christ is not controlling all of me, the chances are very good that He is not controlling any of me. I do not want to be cruel, but I must be honest: Jesus Christ wants to be and must be Lord. He must be head of and Lord of all departments of our lives. We cannot have a girlfriend or a husband or a home or a job shut up in an airtight compartment that Jesus cannot control. If Jesus is not Lord of all of us, we are not real disciples.

3.The Lordship of Christ

The Scriptures do not teach that the person of Jesus Christ nor any of the important offices that God has given Him can be divided or ignored according to the whims of men. Therefore, I must be frank in my feeling that a notable heresy has come into being throughout our evangelical Christian circles—the widely accepted concept that we humans can choose to accept Christ only because we need Him as Savior, and we have the right to postpone our obedience to Him as Lord as long as we want to!

This concept has sprung naturally from a misunderstanding of what the Bible actually says about Christian discipleship and obedience. It is now found in nearly all of our full gospel literature. I confess that I was among those who preached it before I began to pray earnestly, to study diligently and meditate with anguish over the whole matter.

I think the following is a fair statement of what I was taught in my early Christian experience and it certainly needs a lot of modifying and a great many qualifiers to save us from being in error. "We are saved by accepting Christ as our Savior; we are sanctified by accepting Christ as our Lord; we may do the first without doing the second!"

The truth is that salvation apart from obedience is unknown in the sacred Scriptures. Peter makes it plain that we are *"elect according to the foreknowledge of God the Father, through sanctification of the Spirit, unto obedience"* (1 Peter 1:2). What a tragedy that in our day we often hear the gospel appeal made on this kind of basis: "Come to Jesus! You do not have to obey anyone. You do not have to change anything. You do not have to give up anything, alter anything, surrender anything, give back anything—just come to Him and believe in Him as Savior!"

So they come and believe in the Savior. Later on, in a meeting or conference, they will hear another appeal: "Now that you have received Him as Savior, how would you like to take Him as Lord?"

The fact that we hear this everywhere does not make it right. To urge men and women to believe in a divided Christ is bad teaching, for no one can receive half of Christ, or a third of Christ, or a quarter of the person of Christ! We are not saved by believing in an office nor in a work.

I heard well-meaning workers say, "Come and believe on the finished work." That work will not save you. The Bible does not tell us to believe in an office or a work, but to believe on the Lord Jesus Christ Himself, the person who has done that work and holds those offices.

Now, note again, Peter's emphasis on obedience among the scattered and persecuted Christians of his day. It seems most important to me that Peter speaks of his fellow Christians as "obedient children" (1 Peter 1:14). He was not giving them a command or exhortation to be obedient. In effect, he said, "Assuming that you are believers, I therefore gather that you are also obedient. So now, as obedient children, do so and so."

Brethren, I would point out that obedience is taught throughout the entire Bible and that true obedience is one of the toughest requirements of the Christian life. Apart from obedience, there can be no salvation, for salvation without obedience is a self-contradictory impossibility. The essence of sin is rebellion against divine authority.

God said to Adam and Eve, *"But of the tree of the knowledge of good and evil, thou shalt not eat of it: for in the day that thou eatest thereof thou shalt surely die."* (Gen. 2:17) Here was a divine requirement calling for obedience on the part of those who had the power of choice and will. In spite of the strong prohibition, Adam and Eve stretched forth their hands and tasted of the fruit and thus they disobeyed and rebelled, bringing sin upon themselves. Paul writes very plainly and directly in the book of Romans about "one man's disobedience" (Rom. 5:19). This is a stern word by the Holy Spirit through the apostle—by one man's disobedience came the downfall of the human race!

In John's gospel, the Word is very plain and clear that sin is lawlessness, that sin is disobedience to the law of God. Paul's picture of sinners in Ephesians concludes that the people of the world are "the children of disobedience" (Eph. 2:2). Paul certainly means that disobedience characterizes them, conditions them, molds them. Disobedience has become a part of their nature. All of this provides background for the great, continuing question before the human race:

"Who is boss?" This breaks down into a series of three questions: "To whom do I belong?" "To whom do I owe allegiance?" and "Who has authority to require obedience of me?"

Now, I suppose of all the people in the world Americans have the most difficult time in giving obedience to anyone or anything. Americans are supposed to be sons of freedom. We ourselves were the outcropping of a revolt. We spawned a revolution, pouring the tea overboard in the Boston harbor. We made speeches and said, "That sound of the clash of arms is carried on every wind that blows from the Boston Commons" and finally, "Give me liberty or give me death!"

That is in the American blood, and when anyone says, "You owe obedience," we immediately bristle! In the natural sense, we do not take kindly to the prospect of yielding obedience to anyone. In the same sense, the people of this world have a quick and ready answer to the questions: "To whom do I belong?" and "To whom do I owe obedience?" Their answer is: "I belong to myself. No one has authority to require my obedience!"

Our generation makes a great deal out of this, and we give it the name of "individualism." On the basis of our individuality, we claim the right of self-determination. In an airplane, the pilot who sits at the controls determines where that plane is going. He must determine the destination. Now, if God had made us humans to be mere machines, we would not have the power of self-determination. But since He made us in His own image and made us to be moral creatures, He has given us that power of self-determination....

The poet Tennyson must have thought about this for he wrote in his "In Memoriam": "Our wills are ours, we know not how; our wills are ours to make them Thine." Oh, this mystery of a man's free will is far too great for us! Tennyson said, "We know not how." But then he girds himself and continues, "Yes, our wills are ours to make them Thine." And that is the only right we have here to make our wills the wills of God, to make the will of God our will!

We must remember that God is Who He is, and we are what we are. God is the Sovereign and we are the creatures. He is the Creator and therefore He has a right to command us with the obligation that we should obey. It is a happy obligation, I might say, for *"[His] yoke is easy, and [His] burden is light."* (Matt. 11:30)

Now, this is where I raise the point again of our human insistence that Christ may sustain a divided relationship toward us. This is now so commonly preached that to oppose it or object to it means that you are sticking your neck out and you had best be prepared for what comes. But how can we insist and teach that our Lord Jesus Christ can be our Savior without being our Lord? How can we continue to teach that we can be saved without any thought of obedience to our Sovereign Lord?

I am satisfied that when man believes on Jesus Christ, he must believe on the whole Lord Jesus Christ—not making any reservation! I am satisfied that it is wrong to look upon Jesus as a kind of divine nurse to whom we can go when sin has made us sick, and after He has helped us, to say goodbye and go on our own way.

Suppose I slip into a hospital and tell the staff I need a blood transfusion or perhaps an X-ray of my gall bladder. After they have ministered to me and given their services, do I just slip out of the hospital again with a cheery goodbye—as though I owe them nothing and it was kind of them to help me in my time of need? That may sound like a grotesque concept to you, but it does pretty well draw the picture of those who have been taught that they can use Jesus as a Savior in their time of need without owning Him as Sovereign and Lord and without owing Him obedience and allegiance.

The Bible never in any way gives us such a concept of salvation. Nowhere are we ever led to believe that we can use Jesus as a Savior and not own Him as our Lord. He is the Lord, and as the Lord He saves us, because He has all of the offices of Savior and Christ and High Priest and Wisdom and Righteousness and Sanctification and Redemption! He is all of these things and all of these are embodied in Him as Christ the Lord.

My brethren, we are not allowed to come to Jesus Christ as shrewd, clever operators saying, "We will take this and this, but we won't take that!" We do not come to Him as one who, buying furniture for his house, declares: "I will take this table but I don't want that chair"— dividing it up! No, sir! It is either all of Christ or none of Christ! I believe we need to preach again a whole Christ to the world—a Christ who does not need our apologies, a Christ who will not be divided, a Christ who will either be Lord of all or who will not be Lord at all!

4.The Sinner and Salvation

As obedient children,

do not conform to the evil desires you had

when you lived in ignorance.

1 PETER 1:14

Fugitives From Law

I think it is important to agree that true salvation restores the right of a Creator-creature relationship because it acknowledges God's right to our fellowship and communion.

You see, in our time we have over-emphasized the psychology of the sinner's condition. We spend much time describing the woe of the sinner, the grief of the sinner and the great burden he carries. He does have all of these, but we have over-emphasized them until we forget the principal fact—that the sinner is actually a rebel against properly constituted authority! That is what makes sin, *sin.*

We are rebels. We are sons of disobedience. Sin is the breaking of the law and we are in rebellion and we are fugitives from the just laws of God while we are sinners.

By way of illustration, suppose a man escapes from prison. Certainly, he will have grief. He is going to be in pain after bumping logs and stones and fences as he crawls and hides away in the dark. He is going to be hungry and cold and weary. His beard will grow long and he will be tired and cramped and cold—all of these will happen, but they are incidental to the fact that he is a fugitive from justice and a rebel against law.

So it is with sinners. They are certainly heartbroken and they carry a heavy load. They certainly labor and are heavy-laden. The Bible takes full account of these things. But they are incidental to the fact that the reason the sinner is what he is, is because he has rebelled against the laws of God and he is a fugitive from divine judgement.

It is that which constitutes the nature of sin; not the fact that he carries a heavy load of misery and sadness and guilt. These things constitute only the outcropping of the sinful nature, but the root of sin is rebellion against God. Does not the sinner say: "I belong to myself—I owe allegiance to no one unless I choose to give it!" That is the essence of sin.

But thankfully, salvation reverses that and restores the former relationship so that the first thing the returning sinner does is to confess: *"Father, I have sinned against heaven, and before thee, and am no more worthy to be called thy son: make me as one of thy hired servants."* (Luke 15:18–19)

Thus, in repentance, we reverse that relationship and we fully submit to the Word of God and the will of God—as obedient children.

Now that happiness of all the moral creatures lies right here, brethren, in the giving of obedience to God. The Psalmist cried out in Psalm 103:21, *"Bless ye the LORD, all ye his hosts; ye ministers of his, that do his pleasure."*

On the other hand, hell is certainly the world of disobedience. Everything else that may be said about hell may be true, but this one thing is the essence—hell is the world of the rebel! Hell is the Alcatraz for the unconstituted rebels who refuse to surrender to the will of God.

I thank God that heaven is the world of God's obedient children. Whatever else we may say of its pearly gates, its golden streets and its jasper walls, heaven is heaven because children of the Most High God find they are in their normal sphere as obedient moral beings. Jesus said there are fire and worms in hell, but that is not the reason it is hell. You might endure worms and fire, but for a moral creature to know and realize that he is where he is because he is a rebel—that is the essence of hell and judgment. It is the eternal world of all the disobedient rebels who have said, "I owe God nothing!"

This is the time given us to decide. Each person makes his own decision as to the eternal world he is going to inhabit.

This is a serious matter of decision. You do not come to this decision as though it were a matter of being interviewed for a job or getting your diploma at a school. We have no basis to believe that we can come casually and sprightly to the Lord Jesus and say, "I have come for some help, Lord Jesus. I understand that You are the Savior so I am going to believe and be saved and then I am going to turn away and think about the other matters of lordship and allegiance and obedience at some time in the future."

I warn you—you will not get help from Him in that way. The Lord will not save those whom He cannot command. He will not divide His offices. You cannot believe on a half-Christ. We take Him for what He is—the anointed Savior and Lord who is King of kings and Lord of lords! He would not be who He is if He saved us and called us and chose us, without the understanding that He can also guide and control our lives.

Brethren, I believe in the deeper Christian life and experience—oh, yes! But I believe we are mistaken when we try to add the deeper life to an imperfect salvation, obtained imperfectly by an imperfect concept of the whole thing. Under the working of the Spirit of God through such men as Finney and Wesley, no one would ever dare to rise in a meeting and say, "I am a Christian" if he had not surrendered his whole being to God and had taken Jesus Christ as his Lord. It was only then that he could say, "I am saved!"

Today, we let them say they are saved no matter how imperfect and incomplete the transaction, with the proviso that the deeper Christian life can be tacked on at some time in the future.

Can it be that we really think that we do not owe Jesus Christ our obedience? We have owed Him obedience ever since the second we cried out to Him for salvation. If we do not give Him that obedience, I have reason to wonder if we are really converted! I see things and I hear of things that Christian people are doing. As I watch them operate within the profession of Christianity, I do raise the question of whether they have been truly converted.

Brethren, I believe it is the result of faulty teaching to begin with. They thought of the Lord as a hospital and Jesus as chief of staff to fix up poor sinners that had gotten into trouble!

"Fix me up, Lord," they have insisted, "so that I can go on my own way!"

That is bad teaching, brethren. It is filled with self-deception. Let us look unto Jesus our Lord, high, holy, wearing the crowns, Lord of lords and King of all, having a perfect right to command full obedience from all of His saved people!

Our Lord gave us a rule by which we can test our love for Him: "*He that hath my commandments, and keepeth them, he it is that loveth me: and he that loveth me shall be loved of my Father, and I will love him, and will manifest myself to him.... If a man love me, he will keep my words.... He that loveth me not keepeth not my sayings.*" (John 14:21, 23–24)

These words are too plain to need much interpreting. Proof of love for Christ is simply removed altogether from the realm of the feelings and placed in the realm of practical obedience. I think the rest of the New Testament is in full accord with this.

No Salvation Apart from Obedience

The Bible knows nothing of salvation apart from obedience. Paul testified that he was sent to preach "obedience to the faith among all nations." He reminded the Roman Christians that they had been set free from sin because they had "obeyed from the heart that form of doctrine which was delivered you."

In the New Testament there is no contradiction between faith and obedience. Between faith and law-works, yes; between law and grace, yes; but between faith and obedience, not at all.

The Bible recognizes no faith that does not lead to obedience, nor does it recognize any obedience that does not spring from faith. The two are opposite sides of the same coin. If we were to split a coin edgewise, we would destroy both sides and render the whole thing valueless. So faith and obedience are forever joined and each one is without value when separated from the other. The trouble with many of us today is that we are trying to believe without intending to obey.

The message of the Cross contains two elements:

(1) Promises and declarations to be believed, and

(2) Commandments to be obeyed.

Obviously, faith is necessary to the first and obedience to the second. The only thing we can do with a promise or statement of fact is to believe it; it is physically impossible to obey it, for it is not addressed to the will, but to the understanding.

It is equally impossible to believe a command. It is not addressed to our understanding, but to our will. True, we may have faith in its justice; we may have confidence that it is a good and right command, but that is not enough. Until we have either obeyed, or refused to obey, we have not done anything about it yet. To strain to exercise faith toward that which is addressed to our obedience is to get ourselves tangled in a maze of impossibilities.

The doctrine of Christ crucified, and the wealth of truths which cluster around it, have in them this dual content. So the apostle could speak of "obedience to the faith" without talking contradictions. And it can be said, "The gospel is the power of God unto salvation to everyone that believeth", and "He became the author of eternal salvation unto all them that obey him." There is nothing incompatible between these statements when they are understood in the light of the essential unity of faith and obedience.

The weakness in our message today is our overemphasis on faith, with a corresponding underemphasis on obedience. This has been carried so far that "believe" has been made to double for "obey" in the minds of millions of religious persons.

The result is a host of mental Christians whose characters are malformed and whose lives are all out of proportion. Imagination has been mistaken for faith. Belief has been robbed of its moral content and made to be little more than an assent to gospel truth. And all this in the name of orthodoxy.

There is a mental disease fairly familiar to all of us where the patient lives in a world wholly imaginary. It is a play-world, a world of pure fancy, with no objective reality corresponding to it. Everyone knows this except the patient himself. He will argue for his world with all the logic of a sane man, and the pathetic thing is that he is utterly sincere.

So we find Christians who have lived so long in the rarefied air of imagination that it seems next to impossible to relate them to reality. Non-obedience has paralyzed their moral legs and dissolved their backbones, and they slump down in a spongy heap of religious theory, believing everything ardently, but obeying nothing at all.

Indeed, they are deeply shocked at the very mention of the word "obey." To them it smacks of heresy and self-righteousness and is the result of failure to rightly divide the word of truth. Their doctrine of supine inaction is New Testament religion! It is the truth for which the Reformers died! Everything else is legalism and the religion of Cain.

All this we might pass over as merely one more of those things, were it not that this creed of the moral impasse has influenced practically every corner of the Christian world. It has captured Bible schools, has determined the content of evangelistic preaching, and has gone far to decide what kind of Christians we all shall be.

Without doubt the popular misconception of the function of faith, and the failure of our teachers to insist upon obedience, have weakened the Church and retarded revival tragically in the last half-century. The only cure is to remove the cause. This will take some courage, but it will be worth the labor.

5. The Foolishness of Sin

Sin is an Act of Wrong Judgement

The world has divided men into two classes, the stupid good people and the clever wicked ones.

This false classification runs through much of the literature of the last centuries from the classics to the comic strip—from Shakespeare's Polomus, who furnished his son with a set of good but dull moral platitudes, to Capp's Li'l Abner, who would never knowingly do a wrong act but who would rather fall on his head than on his feet because there is more feeling in his feet than in his head.

In the Holy Scriptures, things are quite the opposite. There righteousness is always associated with wisdom and evil with folly. Whatever other factors may be present in an act of wrongdoing, folly is one that is never absent. To do a wrong act a man must for the moment think wrong; he must exercise bad judgment.

If this is true then the devil is creation's prime fool, for when he gambled on his ability to unseat the Almighty, he was guilty of an act of judgment so bad as to be imbecilic. He is said to have had a great amount of wisdom, but his wisdom must have deserted him at the time of his first sin, for he surely grossly underestimated the power of God and as grossly overestimated his own.

The devil is not now pictured in the Scriptures as wise, only as shrewd. We are warned not against his wisdom but against his wiles, something very different.

Sin, I repeat, in addition to anything else it may be, is always an act of wrong judgment.

To commit a sin, a man must for the moment believe that things are different from what they really are; he must confound values; he must see the moral universe out of focus; he must accept a lie as truth and see truth as a lie; he must ignore the signs on the highway and drive with his eyes shut; he must act as if he had no soul and was not accountable for his moral choices.

Sin is never a thing to be proud of. No act is wise that ignores remote consequences, and sin always does. Sin sees only today, or at most tomorrow; never the day after tomorrow, next month or next year. Death and judgment are pushed aside as if they did not exist and the sinner becomes for the time a practical atheist, who by his act denies not only the existence of God but the concept of life after death.

History is replete with examples of men whose intellectual powers were great but whose practical judgment was almost nil: Einstein, for instance, who was a mathematical genius but who could not look after his own bank account and who absent-mindedly ran his little motorboat aground with the excuse that he "must have been thinking about something else."

We can smile at this, but there is nothing humorous about that other class of men who had brilliant minds but whose moral judgment was sadly awry. To this class belong such men as Lucretius, Voltaire, Shelley, Oscar Wilde, Walt Whitman and thousands of others whose names are less widely known.

The notion that the careless sinner is the smart fellow, and the serious-minded Christian, though well-intentioned, is a stupid dolt altogether out of touch with life, will not stand up under scrutiny. Sin is basically an act of moral folly, and the greater the folly the greater the fool.

He is the fountain of all wisdom, but He is more—He is wisdom itself. In Him are all the treasures of wisdom and knowledge hidden away!

It is time the young people of this generation learned that there is nothing smart about wrongdoing and nothing stupid about righteousness. We must stop negotiating with evil. We Christians must stop apologizing for our moral position and start making our voices heard, exposing sin for the enemy of the human race which it surely is, and setting forth righteousness and true holiness as the only worthy pursuits for moral beings.

The idea that sin is modern is false. There has not been a new sin invented since the beginning of recorded history. That new vice that breaks out to horrify decent citizens and worry the police is not really new. Flip open that book written centuries ago and you will find it described there. The reckless sinner, trying to think of some new way to express his love of iniquity, can do no more than imitate others like himself, now long dead. He is not the bright rebel he fancies himself to be, but a weak and stupid fellow who must follow along in the long parade of death toward the point of no return.

If the hoary grey head is a crown of glory when it is found in the way of righteousness, it is a fool's cap when it is found in the way of sin. An old sinner is an awesome and frightening spectacle.

One feels about him much as one feels about the condemned man on his way to the gallows. A sense of numb terror and shock fills the heart. The knowledge that the condemned man was once a red-cheeked boy only heightens the feeling.

And the knowledge that the aged rebel now beyond reclamation once went up to the house of God on a Sunday morning to the sweet sound of church bells makes even the trusting Christian humble and a little bit scared. There but for the grace of God goes he.

I am among those who believe that our Western civilization is on its way to perishing. It has many commendable qualities, most of which it has borrowed from the Christian ethic, but it lacks the element of moral wisdom that would give it permanence. Future historians will record that we of the twentieth century had intelligence enough to create a great civilization but not the moral wisdom to preserve it.

A Foolish Way of Life

Forasmuch as ye know that ye were not redeemed

with corruptible things, as silver and gold,

from your vain conversation received by tradition from your fathers;

but with the precious blood of Christ,

as of a lamb without blemish and without spot.

1 PETER 1:18-19

Peter offers this beautiful symbolism of Jesus Christ as a lamb—a sacrificed lamb. He says, "Ye were redeemed." "Redeemed" means "loosed," not in the sense that you would loose a man bound to a post or loose a horse, but loosed in the legal sense of being freed from legal bondage. It is in the sense that a slave is loosed, is legally declared free. And Peter said, "You are loosed from the vain conversation."

Those who insist so religiously on the text, the letter and syllables, of the *King James Version* ought to listen sometimes to some preachers untangling the *King James* translation for modern listeners. For example, "vain conversation" does not mean what it means now. "Vain" means foolish and "conversation" means a manner of life.

So what Peter said is, "For as much as ye know that ye were not redeemed with corruptible things as silver and gold from your foolish way of life…"

This is a way of life that is morally foolish. It is the sinner's way of life, but God calls it a foolish way, an empty way. It is foolish for several reasons.

The sinner's way is foolish because it *neglects to give God His proper place*. Any way of life, any attitude, any political philosophy, any moral philosophy or speculative philosophy, any kind of thinking in any sphere of human thought or life, any standard of morals adopted or followed by any people, however loosely, that does not give God His proper place is declared by the Lord God Himself to be foolish and empty.

People around us are foolish. Men who went out and got themselves pepped up during a holiday and then the next day suffered with an aching head were not so bad as they were just foolish. It is foolish to treat your body like that. They are doing a morally foolish thing because they do not consider God. No man who has God before his mind would ever swill poison liquor down his throat. Therefore, what people do is foolish.

In efforts of evangelism, some people try to make sinners out of everybody in the sense that they make them out to be vicious and low and wicked. That is not true.

There are sinners who will certainly perish and spend their eternity in hell who are nevertheless courteous, kind, friendly gentlemen, and you would consider it a privilege to live next door to them. They are good neighbors, and thoughtful, but they are living without a thought of God in their minds.

Their way is a foolish way of life because it is a godless way of life. It is not always a morally low way of life, for there are levels of wickedness. But it is a way that does not consider God, and the Bible says it is foolish and ignores reason, for righteousness always has reason on its side.

That was one of the teachings of Plato, that every man reasonably wanted to do the right thing, only that man made mistakes in deciding what the right things were. Ignoring reason was one of the basic tenets of the great Greek thinker. He was thinking, of course, of finer thinking people, but the great masses do not think too much. Reason is always on the side of righteousness.

When it comes to whether I should do something this way or that way, and the first way is wrong, but the second way is right, reason is always on the side of right. It is always illogical to do the wrong thing. Peter said that it is a foolish, illogical way to live, because it ignores God, ignores reason and disregards the moral lessons of history.

Even history is not always accurate. Voltaire (1694-1778) once said, "History is a pack of lies we play on the dead." That was a cynic's statement. The truth is, much can be learned from history. One thing we can learn is that it is always better to be righteous and it is always worse to be evil, to live without a thought of God before our minds. Ignoring moral reasoning is a fool's way of life.

And then the sinner's way of life is foolish because it *assumes there is no final reckoning*. It is like the man who plunges into some activity unaware or refusing to consider that someday he is going to have to pay up. Or like the man or woman who dances into the gray dawn and then fills up with stimulants, goes on dancing into the next dawn and beats himself up and abuses himself. They are having a type of fun but they are fools because they are not considering that there is a day of reckoning. There will be a time when angry Mother Nature will say, "Pay up."

The sinner's way is foolish because he does not believe there is a final reckoning—or if he believes it, he foolishly disregards it, assuming he is just going to be able to shuffle off this mortal coil without getting a reckoning and accounting. Well, he is not.

The way of the sinner is foolish because it assumes that man is a one-world being. If there is anything I'm committed to, it is that man lives on two planes, this world and the world above, the physical and the spiritual, the natural and the divine. Man is not made for one world only, but for two. He is made for this world now and the next world later.

The sinner's way of life takes for granted this life and does not expect to face another world. This person jokes about this world being so terrible because you do not get out of it alive; that is very tragic when you consider that there is another world, but sinners act as if there is not.

The Christian is wise because he has considered the second world. He is wise because he takes into account that he must make a reckoning. He is wise because he has taken into account the moral lessons of history. He has not ignored reason but has given God His right place, allowing himself to be chastened with memories and knowledge of how others lived and what they paid for wrong living.

This Way of Life

Peter says this way of life is received by tradition from our fathers, and the power of this way of life over us derives from two sources.

One source is the approval of the ages. What our fathers did, we are inclined to think is right.

As a young preacher in West Virginia, I preached against tobacco. I still hate it as much as I did then, but I have sense enough to know that it is only a pimple on the body of morality. So I do not preach against tobacco, although I hate it. But in those days, I attacked anything that did not look good, and tobacco was one. I used to tell them they were dirty if they used it and could not be Christians.

Do you know the response to that kind of preaching? White-faced anger. "Do you mean to tell me that my old father, who smoked and chewed until he died, and my grandmother, who smoked a clay pipe until she died, all perished?"

They were sanctifying the ways of their parents and they were on the cool end of a hot stick, which is smoking, because they liked the taste of it, but mainly because it was received as tradition from their fathers. It was sanctified by generation after generation of incense burners, and they did not want me to say a word about it. Not for their sakes, but because it seemed to be reflecting on the traditions of their fathers. I have learned better, and I preach Christ now.

People will justify anything if their fathers did it. Peter said you received this way of life by traditions of your father.

Then the second source that this way of life stems from, or rather gets its power from, is what accords with the fallen tendencies of the human heart. Whatever accords with the fallen tendencies of the human heart you always do without much trouble.

If you do what comes naturally, you will be doing the way of the flesh; you will be doing that which is outside of the normal bodily functions. For there is a certain basic physical naturalness that even our Lord Jesus Christ had. It is perfectly natural to eat; it is perfectly natural to sleep, and so on. I am talking about an immoral kind of life that stems out of fallen nature, and that is easy to do.

For example, it is easy for a child to lie. I remember my first lie and how easy it was and how it got me out of a jam. It was Christmas, and my poor mother, God bless her memory, tried to get something for us children, if nothing but a popcorn ball. This time she found a Barlow knife. I got a Barlow knife, and I thought that was wonderful. When it was time to go back to school, they surrounded me and asked me what I got for Christmas. I felt chagrined to tell them I got a Barlow knife, and nothing else. Therefore, I used my imagination and fixed myself up with the nicest bunch of Christmas presents you ever heard of, and I got out of an embarrassing position by telling a lie.

That came naturally; I did not have to work at it. All I had to do was just open my mouth and nature took its course. Because we have these fallen tendencies, the foolish way of life is easy for us. It is always hard to teach a child to be good; let him alone and he will not be good.

You say, "But my little darling is good naturally." You are going to be surprised one of these days. Your disillusionment is coming; your little darling is one of Adam's wild beasts. And if you did not teach him to be good, he would never be good. If you did not teach him to wash, he would be so dirty you would have to fumigate him once a week. And if you did not teach him to tell the truth, he would lie to music. We are alike in things like that, and the reason your children are good is because you are good and you are teaching them to be good. Do not get it wrong, they did not inherit any goodness; you taught them; and that is to your credit, not theirs. And in turn, by the grace of God, we teach the next generation to be good.

People have to be taught to be good, for they will be bad without teaching, because we all receive it from our fathers by tradition, and it accords with the fallen tendencies of our heart. The honest businessman who conducts his affairs in an honest way is doing what he has learned to do. It would be the natural thing for him to reach out and rake in what he can get his hands on. But he has been trained and taught by religion and morals to be different.

Redeemed

From this fallen way of life we are set free; we are redeemed. A Christian has been delivered from this way of life and from the moral magnetism of those entanglements.

A man once told about some sheep dying during a midwinter in Niagara River. Some of them had died upstream in Niagara, and they either would fall in or be thrown into Niagara River. It was very cold, but the tempestuous Niagara was not frozen, and it carried these dead sheep over the falls. Before the sheep went over the falls, the bald eagles would gather and dive down and ride these carcasses and tear out their flesh. One great eagle after another would fly upstream, land on one, tear with her talons, pull with her great sharp beak, get herself a mouth full of meat and gulp it. Then when they were about to go over the falls, they would leap up gracefully on their broad wings and circle back and repeat the same thing over again.

As it was getting colder, one eagle made a mistake. She rode a little too long the last time, and her talons froze into the wool. When she, confident in her self-assurance, spread her great broad wings to take flight, her talons were frozen into the wool of the sheep and she plunged over to her death along with the carcass she had been feeding on. If somebody could have untangled her talons from the wool, it would have been a kind of redemption, a release.

God has provided a moral release from the tradition of our fathers, the foolish way of life that we see all around us. And it has been done by the act of God in redemption, involving the payment of a ransom for tomorrow. It is not a physical captivity, though it has physical implications for sinners, but it is legal in moral aspects. The ransom price had to be a moral ransom price. It had to be the blood of the Holy One, holy enough for God to accept.

So that moral price was paid, and Peter says, "It was not silver or gold." If I were a slave in a market somewhere in Arabia or the Old South, and I was worth $200 or $5,000, depending upon my age and size and ability, someone might come with a pocket full of gold and buy me and then set me free. Bought free with money, with silver and gold. But when your bondage is not physical, but moral, you cannot buy off moral slaves with money.

So Peter said, "Ye were not redeemed with corruptible things, as silver and gold…but with the precious blood of Christ." This blood of the Lamb is precious because of what it means to God and because of what it means and what it meant to our Lord Jesus Christ, the deathless man who volunteered to die. God does not use words carelessly, and He called the blood of the Lamb precious. And it is precious for what it did for men.

To save you and me from death, everything had been tried. Every kind of sacrifice, every kind of ascetic practice and self-immolation, everything blew out in the moral wind. But there was a man who walked in Galilee and had in His veins only a small amount of blood. The average-sized human being has possibly a gallon and a half of blood. It was not much in the great pool of human blood, but if that did not work, we would have died.

But it worked—the blood of Jesus Christ, God's Son, cleanseth from all sin, and for as much as we know, we are redeemed not with silver or gold but with that precious blood of Jesus Christ.

I wonder how many of us know how precious the blood is that we celebrate? But it is only by the preciousness of the blood that any of us are able or worthy to be considered at all by the fine eye of God, and it is only that knowledge that gives me courage to talk about this holy blood. So I do not say, "You should repent"; I say, "We should repent."

If it had failed us, we would have died. But God raised Jesus from the dead, set Him at His own right hand, took that precious blood and sprinkled it on the Judgment Seat, and that Judgment Seat is a Mercy Seat now.

6. The Importance of Obedience

Faith without deeds is useless.

JAMES 2:20

In Deed and In Truth

It would be a convenient arrangement were we so constituted that we could not talk better than we live. For reasons known to God, however, there seems to be no necessary connection between our speaking and our doing.

Here lies one of the deadliest snares in the religious life. I am afraid we modern Christians are long on talk and short on conduct. We use the language of power, but our deeds are the deeds of weakness.

Our Lord and His apostles were long on deeds. The Gospels depict a Man walking in power, *"who went about doing good, and healing all that were oppressed of the devil; for God was with him."* (Acts 10:38)

The moral relation between words and deeds appears quite plainly in the life and teachings of Christ. He did before He spoke, and the doing gave validity to the speaking.

Luke wrote of *"all that Jesus began both to do and teach,"* (Acts 1:1) and I am sure that the order expressed there is not accidental.

In the Sermon on the Mount, Christ placed doing before teaching: *"Whosoever therefore shall break one of these least commandments, and shall teach men so, he shall be called the least in the kingdom of heaven: but whosoever shall do and teach them, the same shall be called great in the kingdom of heaven."* (Matt. 5:19)

Since in one of its aspects, religion contemplates the invisible, it is easy to understand how it can be erroneously made to contemplate the unreal. The praying man talks of that which he does not see. And fallen human minds tend to assume that what cannot be seen is not of any great importance, and probably not even real, if the truth were known.

So religion is disengaged from practical life and retired to the airy region of fancy where dwell the sweet insubstantial nothings that everyone knows do not exist but that they nevertheless lack the courage to repudiate publicly.

I could wish that this were true only of pagan religions and of the vague and ill-defined quasi-religion of the average man; but candor dictates that I admit it to be true also of much that passes for evangelical Christianity in our times. Indeed, it is more than possible that the gods of the heathen are more real to them than the God of the average Christian.

I sympathize with the mood of the poet Wordsworth when he wrote to the effect that he would rather be a sincere pagan who believed in a god that did not exist, than to be a sophisticated Christian who disbelieved in a God who did.

Unquestionably there is not another institution in the world that talks as much and does as little as the church. Any factory that required as much raw material for so small a finished product would go bankrupt in six months. I have often thought that if one-tenth of one percent of the prayers made in the churches of any ordinary American village on one Sunday were answered, the country would be transformed overnight. But that is just our trouble. We pour out millions of words, and never notice that the prayers are not answered.

I trust it may not be uncharitable to say that we not only do *not* expect our prayers to be answered, but would be embarrassed or even disappointed if they *were*. I think it is not uncommon for Christians to present eloquent petitions to the Lord that they know will accomplish nothing. Some of those petitions they dare present only because they know that is the last that they will hear of the whole thing. Many a wordy brother would withdraw his request quickly enough if he had any intimation that God was taking it seriously.

We settle for words in religion because deeds are too costly. It is easier to pray, "Lord, help me to carry my cross daily" than to pick up the cross and carry it. But since the mere request for help to do something we do not actually intend to do has a certain degree of religious comfort, we are content with repetition of the words.

The practice of substituting words for deeds is not something new. The apostle John saw symptoms of it in his day and warned against it: "*My little children, let us not love in word, neither in tongue; but in deed and in truth. And hereby we know that we are of the truth, and shall assure our hearts before him.*" (1 John 3:18–19).

James also had something to say about the vice of words without deeds: "*If a brother or sister be naked, and destitute of daily food, and one of you say unto them, 'Depart in peace, be ye warmed and filled'; notwithstanding ye give them not those things which are needful to the body; what doth it profit?*" (James 2:15–16)

What then: Shall we take a vow of silence? Shall we cease to pray and sing and write and witness till we catch upon our deeds? No. That would not help. We Christians are left in the world to witness, and while we have breath we must speak to men about God and to God about men. How then shall we escape the snare of words without deeds?

It is simple, though not easy. First, let us say nothing we do not mean. Break the habit of conventional religious chatter. Speak only as we are ready to take the consequences. Believe God's promises and obey His commandments. Practice the truth, and we may with propriety speak the truth. Deeds give body to words. As we do acts of power, our words will take on authority and a new sense of reality will fill our hearts.

The supreme purpose of the Christian religion is to make men like God in order that they may act like God. In Christ the verbs *to be* and *to do* follow each other in that order. True religion leads to moral action. The only true Christian is the practicing Christian.

Such a one is in very reality an incarnation of Christ as Christ is the incarnation of God. This is not in the same degree and fullness of perfection, for there is nothing in the moral universe equal to that awful mystery of godliness that joined God and man in eternal union in the person of the Man Christ Jesus. But as the fullness of the Godhead was and is in Christ, so Christ is in the nature of the one who believes in Him in the manner prescribed in the Scriptures.

God always acts like Himself wherever He may be and whatever He may be doing. When God became flesh and dwelt among us, He did not cease to act as He had been acting from eternity.

"He veiled His deity but He did not void it." The ancient name dimmed down to spare the helpless eyes of mortal men, but as much as was seen was true fire. Christ restrained His powers but He did not violate His holiness. In whatsoever He did He was holy, harmless, separate from sinners and higher than the highest heaven.

In eternity God acted like Himself, and when incarnated in human flesh He still continued in all His conduct to be true to His holiness. He does the same when He enters the nature of a believing man. This is the method by which He makes the redeemed man holy. He enters a human nature at regeneration as He once entered human nature at the incarnation. And he acts as becomes God, using that nature as a medium of expression for His moral perfections.

No Substitute for Action

Cicero, the Roman orator, once warned his hearers that they were in danger of making philosophy a substitute for action instead of allowing it to produce action.

What is true of philosophy is true also of religion. The faith of Christ was never intended to be an end in itself, nor to serve instead of something else. In the minds of some teachers, faith stands in lieu of moral conduct and every inquirer after God must take his choice between the two.

We are presented with the well-known either/or: Either we have faith or we have works, and faith saves while works damn us. Hence the tremendous emphasis on faith and the apologetic, mincing approach to the doctrine of personal holiness in modern evangelism.

This error has lowered the moral standards of the church and helped to lead us into the wilderness where we currently find ourselves.

Rightly understood, faith is not a substitute for moral conduct but a means toward it. The tree does not serve in lieu of fruit but as an agent by which fruit is secured. Fruit, not trees, is the end God has in mind in yonder orchard; so Christlike conduct is the end of Christian faith. To oppose faith to works is to make the fruit the enemy to the tree.

Yet that is exactly what we have managed to do. And the consequences have been disastrous.

A miscalculation in laying the foundation of a building will throw the whole superstructure out of plumb. The error that gave us faith as a substitute for action instead of faith in action has raised up in our day unsymmetrical and ugly temples of which we may well be ashamed. And we shall surely give a strict account for it in the day when Christ judges the secrets of our hearts.

In practice, we may detect the subtle—and often unconscious—substitution when we hear a Christian assure someone that he will "pray over" his problem, knowing full well that he intends to use prayer as a substitute for service. It is much easier to pray that a poor friend's needs may be supplied than to supply them.

James's words burn with irony: *"If a brother or sister be naked, and destitute of daily food, and one of you say unto them, Depart in peace, be ye warmed and filled; notwithstanding ye give them not those things which are needful to the body; what doth it profit?"* (James 2:15–16).

And the mystical John sees also the incongruity involved in substituting religion for action: *"But whoso hath this world's good, and seeth his brother have need, and shutteth up his bowels of compassion from him, how dwelleth the love of God in him? My little children, let us not love in word, neither in tongue; but in deed and in truth. And hereby we know that we are of the truth, and shall assure our hearts before him."* (1 John 3:17–19)

A proper understanding of this whole thing will destroy the false and artificial either/or. Then we will not have less faith but more godly works; not less praying but more serving; not fewer words but more holy deeds; not weaker profession but more courageous possession; not a religion as a substitute for action but religion in faith-filled action.

Keep in mind that the god of this world does not mind if you believe in God. "*Thou believest that there is one God; thou doest well: the devils also believe, and tremble.*" (Jas. 2:19)

The devil believes in God, so you are on the same page as him. He does not even mind if you worship God, provided you also worship the gods of this world. As long as you believe in God as millions of Americans do today and do not make Him the number one exclusive priority in your life, the devil has no issue with you.

The evangelical church today is following the course of the liberal movement and going down the same pathway of compromise. One compromise here, another compromise there, and soon there is very little, if any, difference between the so-called Christian and the man in the world.

Obedience is recognizing God's sovereignty and authority and submitting to it without question and without regard to consequence. True obedience always brings us to a point of no return. This is where faith comes in. We do not have to understand what is happening in order to obey God. We do not need to know the outcome in order to obey God. As a matter of faith and trust, we obey God simply because He is God.

7.The Wisdom of Obedience

Escape Corruption

We can know our present properly only as we know our past, and in that past there occurred something disgraceful and tragic: namely, the loss of our moral character and rebellion against our Creator. That we also lost our happiness is of secondary importance, since it is but a result of our alienation from God and not a part of that alienation.

The primary work of Christ in redemption is to justify, sanctify and ultimately to glorify a company of persons salvaged from the ruin of the human race.

For the convenience of any who may not be familiar with the words used here, I would explain that *justify* means to declare righteous before God; *sanctify* means to make holy; and *glorify* means in effect to remake the entire personality after the image of Christ.

This will fit us to dwell eternally in that heaven about which the Bible speaks and which is both a state of being and a location. In that heaven the ransomed will experience unclouded communion with the Triune God; and that will itself assure unalloyed blessedness.

I have just now used the word "ruin" and associated it with the human race. This is not a figure of speech nor is it an extravagant or irresponsible use of a word. The race lies in ruin, spiritually, morally and physically. History and the daily newspaper testify to our moral ruin. The long parade of gods, both virtuous and obscene, and a thousand varieties of vain and meaningless religious practices declare our spiritual degeneration, while disease, old age and death testify sadly to the completeness of our physical decay.

We inhabit a world suspended halfway between heaven and hell, alienated from one and not yet abandoned to the other. We are unholy by nature and unrighteous by practice. That we are also unhappy, I repeat, is of small consequence.

Our first and imperative duty is to escape the corruption which is in the world as Lot escaped the moral ruin of Sodom. It is of overwhelming importance to us that we should seek the favor of God while it is possible to find it and that we should bring ourselves under the plenary authority of Jesus Christ in complete and voluntary obedience.

To do this is to invite trouble from a hostile world and to incur such unhappiness as may naturally follow. Add to this the temptations of the devil and a lifelong struggle with the flesh, and it will be obvious that we will need to defer most of our enjoyments to a more appropriate time.

Against this background of fact, our childish desire to be happy is seen to be a morally ugly thing, wholly foreign to the Spirit of the Man of Sorrows and contrary to the teaching and practice of His apostles.

Any appeal to the public in the name of Christ that rises no higher than an invitation to tranquility must be recognized as mere humanism with a few words of Jesus thrown in to make it appear Christian. But only that which accords with the spirit and teachings of Christ is truly Christian. Everything else is un-Christian or anti-Christian, no matter whence it emanates.

Strange, is it not, that we dare without shame to alter, to modulate the words of Christ while speaking for Christ to the very ones for whom He died?

Christ calls men to carry a cross; we call them to have fun in His name. He calls them to forsake the world; we assure them that if they but accept Jesus the world is their oyster. He calls them to suffer; we call them to enjoy all the bourgeois comforts modern civilization affords.

He calls them to self-abnegation and death; we call them to spread themselves like green bay trees or perchance even to become stars in a pitiful fifth-rate religious zodiac. He calls them to holiness; we call them to a cheap and tawdry happiness that would have been rejected with scorn by the least of the Stoic philosophers.

In a world like this, with conditions being what they are, what should a serious-minded Christian do? The answer is easy to give but hard to follow.

First, accept the truth concerning yourself. You do not go to a doctor to seek consolation but to find out what is wrong and what to do about it. Seek the kingdom of God and His righteousness. Seek through Jesus Christ a right relation to God and then insist upon maintaining a right relationship to your fellow man. Set about reverently to amend your doings. Magnify God, mortify the flesh, simplify your life. Take up your cross and learn of Jesus Christ to die to this world that He may raise you up in due time.

If you will do these things in faith and love, you will know peace, but it will be the peace of God that passes all understanding. You will know joy, but it will be the joy of resurrection, not the irresponsible happiness of men who insist on carnal enjoyments. You will know the comfort of the indwelling Spirit which will often spring up like a well of water in the desert, not because you have sought it but have sought rather to do the will of God at any price.

We can afford to suffer now; we'll have a long eternity to enjoy ourselves. And our enjoyment will be valid and pure, for it will come in the right way at the right time.

The Way of Greatness

"Whosoever will be great among you, let him be your minister," said our Lord (Matt. 20:20-28). From these words we may properly conclude (and the context strongly supports the conclusion) that there is nothing wrong with the desire to be great, provided

(1) we seek the right kind of greatness;

(2) we allow God to decide what is greatness;

(3) we are willing to pay the full price that greatness demands, and

(4) we are content to wait for the judgment of God to settle the whole matter of who is great at last.

It is vitally important, however, that we know what Christ meant when He used the word *great* in relation to men, and His meaning cannot be found in the lexicon or dictionary. Only when viewed in its broad theological setting is it understood aright.

No one whose heart has had a vision of God, however brief or imperfect that vision may have been, will ever consent to think of himself or anyone else as being great. The sight of God, when He appears in awesome majesty to the wondering eyes of the soul, will bring the worshiper to his knees in fear and gladness and fill him with such an overwhelming sense of divine greatness that he must spontaneously cry *"Only God is great!"*

All this being true, still God Himself applies the word *great* to men, as when the angel tells Zacharias that the son who is to be born *"shall be great in the sight of the Lord,"* or as when Christ speaks of some who shall be great in the kingdom of heaven.

Obviously, there are two kinds of greatness recognized in the Scriptures—an absolute, uncreated greatness belonging to God alone; and a relative and finite greatness achieved by or bestowed upon certain friends of God and sons of faith, who by obedience and self-denial sought to become as much like God as possible. It is of this latter kind of greatness that we speak.

To seek greatness is not wrong in itself. Men were once made in the image of God and told to subdue the earth and have dominion. Man's desire to rise above his present state and to bring all things under subjection to him may easily be the blind impulse of his fallen nature to fulfill the purpose for which he was created. Sin has perverted this natural instinct as it has all others. Men have left their first estate, and in their moral ignorance invariably look for greatness where it is not, and seek to attain it in ways that are always vain and often downright iniquitous.

By the life He lived and the words He spoke, our Lord cleared up the confusion that existed concerning human greatness. That is, He cleared it up for all who are willing to hear His words and to accept His life as a model for their own.

The essence of His teaching is that true greatness lies in character, not in ability or position. Men in their blindness had always thought that superior talents made a man great, and so the vast majority believe today. To be endowed with unusual abilities in the field of art or literature or music or statecraft, for instance, is thought to be in itself evidence of greatness, and the man thus endowed is hailed as a great man. Christ taught, and by His life demonstrated, that greatness lies deeper.

"The princes of the Gentiles," He called the men who gained political power by their superior talents, or who inherited their position of dominion over their fellow men. It is obvious that He was not impressed by that kind of greatness, for He drew a sharp line between it and true greatness. *"It shall not be so among you,"* He told His followers. A new and radical conception of greatness had been introduced.

While a few philosophers and religionists of pre-Christian times had seen the fallacy in man's idea of greatness and had exposed it, it was Christ who located true greatness and showed how it could be attained. *"Whosoever will be great among you, let him be your minister; and whosoever will be chief among you, let him be your servant."* It is that simple and that easy—and that difficult.

The ease and the simplicity are there for anyone to see. We have but to follow Christ in service to the human race, a selfless service that asks only to serve, and greatness will be ours. That is all, but it is too much, for it runs counter to all that is Adam in us. Adam still feels the instinct for dominion; he hears deep within him the command: *"Replenish the earth, and subdue it,"* and he does not take kindly to the command to serve.

And there lies the confusion, the contradiction, that sin has brought, for sin is the trouble after all, and sin must go. Sin must go and Adam must give way to Christ; so says our Lord in effect. By sin men have lost dominion, even their very right to it, until they win it back by humble service. Though redeemed from death and hell by the vicarious labor of Christ on the cross, still the right to have dominion must be won by each man separately. Each must fulfill a long apprenticeship as a servant before he is fit to rule.

After Christ had served (and His service included death), God highly exalted Him and gave Him a name above every name. As a man He served and won His right to have dominion.

Christ found it easy to serve because He had no sin. Nothing in Him rebelled against the lowliest ministrations our fallen nature required. He knew where true greatness lay, and we do not. We try to climb up to higher positions when God has ordained that we go down.

"Whosoever will be chief among you, let him be your servant."

Peace in God

It is ironic that this generation, which more than any other in history preaches the brotherhood of man, is also the generation most torn by unbrotherly strife.

War, either cold or hot, has plagued the earth incessantly from the day Cain slew Abel to the present moment. But never before in the history of the race have there been such deep hatreds, such alienation of hearts, such suspicion, such bitter accusations, such threats, such frenetic competition to perfect and pile up horror weapons capable of wiping out whole cities instantaneously.

For the first time in human history the language of generals and statesmen is beginning to sound like the Apocalypse, and the frightening thing is that science has given the war lords the power to bring apocalyptic destruction upon the world.

Science, the sweet-talking goddess which but a short time ago smilingly disposed of the Bible as a trustworthy guide and took the world by the hand to lead it into a man-made millennium, has turned out to be a dragon capable of destroying that same world with a flick of her fiery tail.

The world talks of peace, and by *peace* it means the absence of war. What it overlooks is that there is another meaning of the word, namely, tranquility of heart, and without that kind of peace the peace of the world will continue to be but an unattainable dream. As long as peace between nations continues to depend upon the shifting moods of choleric old men, filled with hatred and frustration at their approaching dissolution, and who are ready to pull the world down with them into the bottomless pit—just that long will there be no peace among nations.

In spite of all the books lately published, inward tranquility cannot be found on the earth. Peace has fled the halls of learning, and if found at all, is found now among the lowly. Once men sought philosophy as a way of life; from her they learned to be satisfied with their lot, resigned and patient with men and with nature. Socrates, Marcus Aurelius, Epictetus—these could teach Khrushchev, Nasser and Tito, but from such as these such as they will not learn. Hate, greed, megalomania and the mad ambition that in every generation "o'erleaps itself" drive the leaders of nations savagely to kill and destroy for the furtherance of their incredibly wicked ends.

But we need not look at kings and generals to discover the bankruptcy of the world. Go but to the corner store; drive your car down a busy street; take a quick glance at the crowds getting on or off a bus; try to buy a house or to sell one; in short, engage in any common pursuit and the secret is immediately out. Among the sons of fallen men there is no peace of mind or of heart.

True peace is a gift of God, and today it is found only in the minds of innocent children and in the hearts of trustful Christians. "Peace I leave with you," said our Lord at the close of His earthly ministry; my peace I give unto you: not as the world giveth, give I unto you. Let not your heart be troubled, neither let it be afraid."

It is time that we Christians awake to the fact that the world cannot help us in anything that matters. Not the educators nor the legislators nor the scientists can bring us tranquility of heart, and without tranquility whatever else they give us is useless at last. For more than half a lifetime I have listened to their promises, and they have so far failed to make good on a single one of them. To turn to God is now the only reasonable thing to do; we have no second choice. "Lord, to whom shall we go? Thou hast the words of eternal life."

It is an ironic thought too that fallen men, though they cannot fulfill their promises, are always able to make good on their threats.

For decades they have been promising us a warless world where peace and brotherhood shall sit quiet as a brooding dove. All they have given us is the control of a few diseases and the debilitating comforts of push-button living. These have extended our lives a little longer so we are now able to stay around to see our generation die one by one. When the riper years come upon us. they retire us by compulsion and turn us out to clutter up a world that has no place for us, a world that does not understand us and that we do not understand.

But A-bombs and H-bombs and intercontinental missiles and atomic submarines able to belch irradiant death upon us from below the surface of the sea—these they have perfected and stand ready to use any time the undisciplined temper of some president or prime minister gets sufficiently out of hand.

In view of all this, how wise is the man who has made the God of Jacob his hope and has taken refuge in the Rock of Ages. He has repudiated a world that can make good only on its threats, and has fled for refuge to the Savoir who waits long before carrying out His threats but is ready any moment to fulfill a promise.

Maybe the great of the world have underestimated the Christian after all. When the big day comes, he may stand like Abraham above the burning plain and watch the smoke rising from the cities that forgot God. Neither science nor learning can quench the fires of judgment in that day, but a Christian can steal a quick look at Calvary and know that his judgment is past.

8.Hear the Voice of God

God will speak to us if we read and study and obey the Word of God. But when He does speak, we should speak back to Him in prayer and devotion. That which we speak to Him is important, as we can see in the book of Psalms. Here is a man—an inspired man—speaking back to God!

In a similar way, that is why the great devotional literature is so helpful to us. God has spoken to His saints and they have spoken back to Him, and in His wisdom, He has preserved many of these examples for us.

We are taking some suggestions from a 600-year-old volume, *The Cloud of Unknowing*, written by an anonymous saint of God. It was his premise that many among us are common Christians, while others press on into "special" and "singular" and "perfect" stages of Christian life and experience.

"The first three of these may be begun and ended in this life," he wrote. "You can enter into perfection but you cannot enter in fully because the fourth may by grace be begun here but it shall last without end in the bliss of heaven."

I believe that is a perfect response to Paul's expression that *"I count not myself to have apprehended, neither were already perfect; but let us therefore as many as be perfect be thus minded" (paraphrase from Philippians 3:12-15)*. Here is the blessed contradiction—we have entered into perfection, but we have not yet gone all the way!

The Apostle Paul was stretching forth in that light and radiance which shines more and more unto the perfect day. He said that all will be raised from the dead, but he pressed forward because of God's promise of a better resurrection out from among the dead.

"Not as though I had already attained, either were already perfect: but I follow after ... forgetting those things which are behind." (Philippians 3:12-13)

In the light of Paul's commitment and desire, what shall we say about the shameful mediocrity of the average or common Christian in daily life and experience? What are his reasons for not moving forward in the plan and will of God for his life?

Settling For Mediocrity

First, consider the definition of the word common. It means just plain ordinary—of common rank or quality or ability.

A common Christian is one who is of ordinary quality and ability. He is not distinguished by superiority of any kind. He has begun. He does believe. Perhaps he carries a Bible. But he is not distinguished for spiritual attainment.

I must leave it to each of you whether this is a description of your own kind of spirituality as a Christian. Perhaps you are of just common quality, not distinguished in your Christian life in any way. As a result no one will ever want to consult you for guidance or help. No one will ever want to quote you about the things of God.

Mediocre—most Christians are mediocre!

Actually, I hate the word—mediocre! I get no pleasure out of using it, but I think I am telling the truth when I say that it describes many Christians.

The word mediocre comes from two Latin words and literally means "halfway to the peak." This makes it an apt description of the progress of many Christians. They are halfway up to the peak. They are not halfway to heaven but halfway up to where they ought to be, halfway between the valley and the peak. They are morally above the hardened sinner but they are spiritually beneath the shining saint.

Many have settled down right there, and the tragedy is that years ago some of you said, "I am not going to fail God. I am going to push my way up the mountain until I am at the top of the peak, at the highest possible point of experience with God in this mortal life!"

But you have done nothing about it. If anything, you have lost spiritual ground since that day. You are now a halfway Christian! You are lukewarm, neither hot nor cold. You are halfway up to the peak, halfway to where you could have been if you had pressed on.

Do we really think that this halfway Christian life is the best that Christ offers—the best that we can know? In the face of what Christ offers us, how can we settle for so little? Think of all that He offers us by His blood and by His Spirit, by His sacrificial death on the cross, by His resurrection from the dead, by His ascension to the right hand of the Father, by His sending forth of the Holy Ghost!

I know that many are settling for far less than God is waiting to give. They try to stay happy by adding something to their religion that tickles their carnality from the outside. They introduce converted cowboys and half-converted movie actors, and I think they would even stoop to talking horses and gospel dogs to be able to join in saying, "We had a wonderful time!" They will pay a big price to feature some "ninety-day wonder" so they can get the people to crowd in.

Such as these are mediocre Christians. They have not gained the heights where they can feel the warmth of the sun and yet they are not far enough down to be frozen in the valley.

God is certainly not honored by our arrested development—our permanent halfway spiritual condition. We honor and please Him by going on to full maturity in Christ. We all know that this is what the Bible teaches. Read your New Testament again and you will agree that mediocrity in the Christian life is not the highest that Jesus offers.

Devotion Does Not Consider Consequences

Why, then, are we such common Christians? Why have we settled for such shallow pleasures, those little joys that tickle the saintlets and charm the fancy of the carnal?

It is because we once heard a call to take up the cross, and instead of following toward the heights, we bargained with the Lord like a Maxwell Street huckster. We started asking selfish questions and laying down our own conditions.

We had seen the finger of God beckoning. We had been stirred by His Spirit, and all aglow with desire, we considered going up to the mountain. We felt an urge to be spent for Christ, to live as near to spiritual perfection as it is possible in this life.

However, instead of going on we started asking questions. We began to bicker and bargain with God about His standards for spiritual attainment.

This is plain truth, not about unbelieving "liberals" but about those who have been born again. We have His life—and yet when He calls us to the heights, we begin to quibble and bargain.

"Lord, *what will it cost me*?" we ask. "I want to go on, but I want to know what it will cost me!"

I am convinced that anyone who brings up the question of consequences in the Christian life is only a mediocre and common Christian. He seems to have completely forgotten that the cross is involved at this point.

Jesus Himself plainly said, *"Take up [your] cross daily, and follow me"* (Luke 9:23), and *"If any man serve me, let him follow me; and where I am, there shall also my servant be: if any man serve me, him will my Father honor."* (John 12:26) Jesus said that!

So, the devoted and committed person who takes the cross and follows the Lord does not ask what the consequences will be, neither does he argue about God's plan and God's wisdom.

I have known some who were interested in the deeper life, but hesitated for fear of what such a decision would cost in time, in money, in effort or perhaps in the matter of friendships. These are some of the areas that hinder us.

Now, I do not mean to put down the value and meaning of dear friendships. Human friendships can have a beautiful character that will carry over into the world to come. But the point is that if we ask questions about losing friends when the Lord is dealing with us about spiritual blessing and victory, we are not worthy to be among the saints.

Another question that people ask of the Lord when He calls them to move forward is: "*Will it be safe?*"

This question comes out of our constant bleating about "security" and our everlasting desire for safety above all else.

We ought to be prepared to the fact that faith has a disturbing element within it. In the days of Luther, when it cost something to be a Christian, the old Lutherans said: "Faith is a perturbing thing."

Dare we face the fact that the Word of God more often than not puts us in a place of peril, rather than settling us down easily in a place of security? But most Christians in our day want to dictate to God—they will not accept a place of peril. They do not want to trust.

Some of us have had a delightful experience with a Christian brother from England. He had formerly made money in business and never went anywhere without taking large sums with him. But the Holy Spirit began dealing with him about God's provision and God's resources. Sharing his experience with us, he said: "My wife and I have committed everything to God. We don't even own a house. We have no regular income. I do the work of an evangelist and we are just out doing God's will.

"It is not at all unusual now for us to get in our car and travel several hundred miles with only ten dollars for expenses and not knowing what the next step will be," he told us. "God is spending us. He will not let us down but He is holding us to it so that we will never be able to get our earthly roots in again."

This is the language of the confident Christian who is going on with God. That question, "Is it safe?" is an ignoble question. What is the difference whether it is safe or not as long as He is our Lord?

A third question that we want Him to answer for us is, "*Will it be convenient?*"

What must our Lord think of us if His work and His witness depend upon the convenience of His people? The truth is that every advance that we make for God and for His cause must be made at our inconvenience. If it does not inconvenience us at all, there is no cross in it!

If we have been able to reduce spirituality to a smooth pattern and it costs us nothing—no disturbance, no bother and no element of sacrifice in it—we are not getting anywhere with God. We have stopped and pitched our unworthy tent halfway between the swamp and the peak.

We are mediocre Christians!

Was there ever a cross that was convenient? Was there ever a convenient way to die? I have never heard of any, and judgment is not going to be a matter of convenience, either! Yet we look around for convenience, thinking we can reach the mountain peak conveniently and without trouble or danger to ourselves.

Actually, mountain climbers are always in peril, and they are always advancing at their inconvenience.

Still another of those huckster questions that we ask when we hear the voice of Jesus calling us onward is this: *"Will it be fun?"*

I am sure you know my reaction to this one. No one who asks this question about spiritual advance will ever be anything but a common Christian. He will be mediocre until he dies. He will never be recognized in any way for significant spiritual qualities, and he will never be outstanding for any gifts of the Holy Ghost.

It is because there are so many of these ignoble saintlets, these miniature editions of the Christian way, demanding that Christianity must be fun, that distinct organizations have been launched to give it to them. Yes, there are organizations that exist for the sole purpose of mixing religion and fun for our Christian young people.

In answer to this, I happen to know that young people can be just as responsible before God as older people. The youth who meets Jesus and is converted is just as ready and responsible for inconvenience and cost to himself as is the man of seventy.

Jesus Christ never offered amusement or entertainment for His disciples, but in our day we have to offer both if we are going to get the people—because they are common Christians.

Because fun and popularity seem to go hand in hand, some of the indecisive ask, "Oh Lord, *will I still be popular* if I follow all the way?"

Ah, the weaklings, the weaklings! They must have the approval and support of the group because they are afraid of standing alone. They want to be able to fit in, seeking a guarantee of solidarity in order to bolster one another in the face of sagging courage. Some just cannot stand alone, and when they ask, "Is it popular?" they are avoiding the path of standing alone for God.

I was converted by the grace of God when I was seventeen years old, and there was no other Christian in my home. It was in the city of Akron and my family took in boarders. We had a house full of people at all times, and yet, in the matter of my faith, I was completely alone.

I must not leave the impression that I stood as nobly as Stephen in the book of Acts, but I did stand—and it was tough to stand alone. No one else wanted to go to church. No one wanted to pray at the table. No one wanted to read the Bible, but by the good grace of God, I stood alone and I have always been able to thank God for the results.

My mother and father were both converted, as well as two of my sisters. A brother-in-law was converted before he died, and several others came to know the Savior.

What if I had argued: "Lord, is it popular? What will it cost me?" Those persons would never have met the Lord. God stands willing to give us His help by His grace and mercy.

Many who are God's children have probably hesitated at times and tried to bargain with God. They have known Him in conversion. They know that the change came—and yet they bear the marks of mediocrity. But the important thing is this—they are not at the end of God's love!

It is one of the devil's oldest tricks to discourage the saints by causing them to look back at what they were. No one will make progress with God until he lifts up his eyes and stops looking at himself. We are not to spend our time looking back and looking in—we are told to look forward!

Our Lord is more than able to take care of our past. He pardons instantly and forgives completely. His blood makes us worthy—all we are and all we have is by the forgiving love of God!

The goodness of God is infinitely more wonderful than we will ever be able to comprehend. If the root of the matter is in you and you are born again, God is prepared to start with you where you are, and He will not belittle you for your years of common Christianity!

9.Progressing

Motion without Progress is Wasteful

There is probably not another field of human activity where there is so much waste as in the field of religion.

It is altogether possible to waste an hour in church or even in a prayer meeting. Popular "attend the church of your choice" signs have lately been appearing everywhere. They may have some small value if they do no more than remind a materialistic civilization that this world is not all and that there are some treasures that cannot be bought with money. Yet we must not forget that a man may attend church for a lifetime and be none the better for it.

In the average church we hear the same prayers repeated each Sunday year in and year out with, one would suspect, not the remotest expectation that they will be answered. It is enough, it seems, that they have been uttered. The familiar phrase, the religious tone, the emotionally loaded words have their superficial and temporary effect, but the worshiper is no nearer to God, no better morally and no surer of heaven than he was before.

Yet every Sunday morning for twenty years he goes through the same routine allowing two hours for him to leave his house, sit through a church service and return to his house again. He has wasted more than 170 twelve-hour days with this exercise in futility.

The writer to the Hebrews says that some professed Christians were marking time and getting nowhere. They had had plenty of opportunity to grow, but they had not grown; they had had sufficient time to mature, yet they were still babes. He exhorted them to leave their meaningless religions round and press on to perfection (Heb. 5:11-6:3).

It is possible to have motion without progress, and this describes much of the activity among Christians today. It is simply lost motion.

In God there is motion, but never wasted motion; He always works toward a predetermined end. Being made in His image, we are by nature constituted so that we are justifying our existence only when we are working with a purpose in mind. Aimless activity is beneath the worth and dignity of a human being. Activity that does not result in progress toward a goal is waste.

Yet most Christians have no clear end toward which they are striving. On the endless religious merry-go-round, they continue to waste time and energy, of which, God knows, they never had much and have less each hour. This is a tragedy worthy of the mind of an Aeschylus or a Dante.

Back of this tragic waste there is usually one of three causes: The Christian is either ignorant of the Scriptures, unbelieving, or disobedient.

I think most Christians are simply uninstructed. They may have been talked into the kingdom when they were only half-ready. Any convert made within the last thirty years was almost certainly told that he had but to take Jesus as his personal Savior and all would be well. Possibly some counselor may have added that he now had eternal life and would most surely go to heaven when he died—if indeed the Lord does not return and carry him away in triumph before the unpleasant moment of death arrives.

After that first hurried entrance into the kingdom there is usually not much more said. The new convert finds himself with a hammer and a saw and no blueprint. He has not the remotest notion what he is supposed to build, so he settles down to the dull routine of polishing his tools once each Sunday and putting them back in their box.

Sometimes, however, the Christian wastes his efforts because of unbelief. Possibly we are all guilty of this to some degree. In our private prayers and in our public services we are forever asking God to do things that He either has already done or cannot do because of our unbelief.

We plead for Him to speak when He has already spoken and is at that very moment speaking. We ask Him to come when He is already present and waiting for us to recognize Him. We beg the Holy Spirit to fill us while all the time we are preventing Him by our doubts.

Of course, the Christian can hope for no manifestation of God while he lives in a state of disobedience. Let a man refuse to obey God on some dear point, let him set his will stubbornly to resist any commandment of Christ, and the rest of his religious activities will be wasted.

He may go to church for fifty years to no profit. He may tithe, teach, preach, sing, write or edit or run a Bible conference till he gets too old to navigate and have nothing but ashes at the last. "To obey is better than sacrifice."

I need only add that all this tragic waste is unnecessary. The believing Christian will relish every moment in church and will profit by it. The instructed, obedient Christian will yield to God as the clay to the potter, and the result will be not waste but glory everlasting.

Move Forward!

I have long resisted and argued against the assumption that all Christians are alike and that there are no distinctions that can be made between them. "All Christians are saints in God's eyes and that is the end of the matter!" I have been told.

I am acquainted with all of the arguments, but they do not satisfy me in the light of the words of Jesus and the teachings of the apostles. I still think that we must preach and instruct and urge men and women who are toiling along in average and common Christian ways to move forward and claim spiritual victory, which they have not yet known.

If all Christians are alike in standing and state, why did Jesus Christ talk about three distinctions in the Christian life: "some thirty, some sixty and some a hundredfold" (see Matthew 13:8, 23)? Why did He say that some will be qualified to rule over many cities and others over few cities? Why did He teach that some should have higher positions than others in the kingdom of God?

If we are all alike and have arrived at the same place and state, why did the Apostle Paul tell the Philippian Christians: *"I have suffered the loss of all things, and do count them but dung, that I may win*

Christ, and be found in him. ... That I may know him, and the power of his resurrection ... being made conformable unto his death; If by any means I might attain unto the resurrection of the dead" (Philippians 3:8-11)?

Have you ever pondered the full meaning of the much-quoted verse in the Old Testament, Proverbs 4:18: *"The path of the just is as the shining light, that shineth more and more unto the perfect day"*?

I have compared this verse in a number of translations. Goodspeed says, "The path of the righteous is like the light of the dawn that shines ever more brightly until the day is full." Rotherham says, "The path of the righteous is like the light of the dawn going on and brightening unto a more radiant day."

This is an inspired utterance concerning a true relationship with God. Through it, the writer is saying to us that when a person becomes a Christian, the sun comes up. Then, his experience along the path should be like the appearing of the dawn and the glowing of the light, which shineth more and more unto the perfect day.

Christians are very fond of this verse. They memorize it, they quote it—but they don't believe it! If they really believed it, they would enter into this experience— "that shineth more and more unto the perfect day"!

I am of the opinion that we cannot experience that which we have not believed. This is the reason why many Christians remain about where they are—day after day, week after week, year after year. Time moves along, and special revival speakers come and go. As a result, we have little spells in which we hope to do better. But if we are honest, we must admit that most Christians stay mired down right where they are.

The sad thing is that there are many in our churches who do not have a long time to live. They have grown old and yet they are not one inch farther up the mountain than they were on that day when the sun first arose on them in conversion. In fact, some are not even as far advanced along the way with God as they were a few years ago!

It is a sad truth that they have already known a day in the past when their faith was keener, their love warmer, the tears nearer the surface, their love of prayer greater, purity and separation brighter, and the principle within more marked than it is now.

If these things are true, I can only conclude that these are "common" Christians—men and women who do not hear the Lord speaking to them as they should.

Complacency, a Deadly Foe

The complacency of Christians is the scandal of Christianity.

Time is short, and eternity is long. The end of all things is at hand. Man has proved himself morally unfit to manage the world in which he has been placed by the kindness of the Almighty. He has jockeyed himself to the edge of the crater and cannot go back, and in terrible fear he is holding his breath against the awful moment when he will be plunged into the inferno.

In the meantime, a company of people exist on the earth who claim to have the answer to all life's major questions. They claim to have found the way back to God, release from their sins, life everlasting and a sure guarantee of heaven in the world to come.

These are the Christians. They declare that Jesus Christ is very God of very God, made flesh to dwell among us. They insist that He is the Way, the Truth and the Life. They testify that He is to them Wisdom, Righteousness, Sanctification and Redemption, and they steadfastly assert that He will be to them the Resurrection and the Life for eternity to come.

These Christians know, and when pressed will admit, that their finite hearts have explored but a pitifully small part of the infinite riches that are theirs in Christ Jesus.

They read the lives of the great saints whose fervent desire after God carried them far up the mountain toward spiritual perfection. For a brief moment they may yearn to be like these fiery souls, whose light and fragrance still linger in the world where they once lived and laboured.

But the longing soon passes. The world is too much with them and the claims of their earthly lives are too insistent. So, they settle back to live their ordinary lives, and accept the customary as normal. After a while they manage to achieve some kind of inner content and that is the last we hear of them.

This contentment with inadequate and imperfect progress in the life of holiness is, I repeat, a scandal in the Church of the Firstborn. The whole weight of Scripture is against such a thing. The Holy Spirit constantly seeks to arouse the complacent. "Let us go on" is the word of the Spirit.

The Apostle Paul embodies this in his noble testimony as found in his Philippian epistle: "*But what things were gain to me, those I counted loss for Christ. Yea doubtless, and I count all things but loss for the excellency of the knowledge of Christ Jesus my Lord: for whom I have suffered the loss of all things, and do count them but dung, that I may win Christ ... that I may know him, and the power of his resurrection ... but this one thing I do, forgetting those things which are behind, and reaching forth unto those things which are before, I press toward the mark for the prize of the high calling of God in Christ Jesus.*"

If we accept this as the sincere expression of a normal Christian, I do not see how we can justify our own indifference toward spiritual things. There is every reason why we should all go forward in our Christian lives and no reason why we should not. Let us go on.

10.How To Make Spiritual Progress

Should someone feel a desire to make definite progress in the life of Christ, what can he do to get on with it?

Here are a few suggestions:

1. Strive to get beyond mere pensive longing. Set your face like a flint and begin to put your life in order. Every man is as holy as he really wants to be. But the want must be all-compelling.

Tie up the loose ends of your life. Begin to tithe; institute family prayer; pay up your debts as far as possible and make some kind of frank arrangement with every creditor you cannot pay immediately; make restitution as far as you can; set aside time to pray and search the Scriptures; surrender wholly to the will of God. You will be surprised and delighted with the results.

2. Put away every un-Christian habit from you. If other Christians practice it without compunction, God may be calling you to come nearer to Him than these other

Christians care to come. Remember the words, "Others may, you cannot." Do not condemn or criticize, but seek a better way. God will honor you.

3. Get Christ Himself in the focus of your heart and keep Him there continually.

Only in Christ will you find complete fulfilment. In Him you may be united to the Godhead in conscious, vital awareness. Remember that all of God is accessible to you through Christ. Cultivate His knowledge above everything else on earth.

4. Throw your heart open to the Holy Spirit and invite Him to fill you. He will do it.

Let no one interpret the Scriptures for you in such a way as to rule out the Father's gift of the Spirit. Every man is as full of the Spirit as he wants to be. Make your heart a vacuum and the Spirit will rush in to fill it.

Nowhere in the Scriptures nor in Christian biography was anyone ever filled with the Spirit who did not know that he had been, and nowhere was anyone filled who did not know when. And no one was ever filled gradually.

5. Be hard on yourself and easy on others. Carry your own cross but never lay one on the back of another. Begin to practice the presence of God. Cultivate the fellowship of the Triune God by prayer, humility, obedience and self-abnegation.

Let any Christian do these things and he will make rapid spiritual progress. There is every reason why we should all go forward in our Christian lives and no reason why we should not. Let us go on.

The New Life

All unannounced and mostly undetected there has come in modern times a new cross into popular evangelical circles. It is like the old cross, but different: the likenesses are superficial; the differences, fundamental.

From this new cross has sprung a new philosophy of the Christian life, and from that new philosophy has come a new evangelical technique—a new type of meeting and a new kind of preaching. This new evangelism employs the same language as the old, but its content is not the same and its emphasis not as before.

The old cross would have no truck with the world. For Adam's proud flesh it meant the end of the journey. It carried into effect the sentence imposed by the law of Sinai.

The new cross is not opposed to the human race; rather, it is a friendly pal and, if understood aright, it is the source of oceans of good clean fun and innocent enjoyment.

It lets Adam live without interference. His life motivation is unchanged; he still lives for his own pleasure, only now he takes delight in singing choruses and watching religious movies instead of singing bawdy songs and drinking hard liquor. The accent is still on enjoyment, though the fun is now on a higher plane morally if not intellectually.

The new cross encourages a new and entirely different evangelistic approach. The evangelist does not demand abnegation of the old life before a new life can be received. He preaches not contrasts but similarities. He seeks to key into public interest by showing that Christianity makes no unpleasant demands; rather, it offers the same thing the world does, only on a higher level. Whatever the sin-mad world happens to be clamoring after at the moment is cleverly shown to be the very thing the gospel offers, only the religious product is better.

The new cross does not slay the sinner, it redirects him. It gears him into a cleaner anal jollier way of living and saves his self-respect. To the self-assertive it says, "Come and assert yourself for Christ." To the egotist it says, "Come and do your boasting in the Lord." To the thrill-seeker it says, "Come and enjoy the thrill of Christian fellowship." The Christian message is slanted in the direction of the current vogue in order to make it acceptable to the public.

The philosophy back of this kind of thing may be sincere but its sincerity does not save it from being false. It is false because it is blind. It misses completely the whole meaning of the cross.

The old cross is a symbol of death. It stands for the abrupt, violent end of a human being. The man in Roman times who took up his cross and started down the road had already said goodbye to his friends. He was not coming back. He was going out to have it ended. The cross made no compromise, modified nothing, spared nothing; it slew all of the man, completely and for good. It did not try to keep on good terms with its victim. It struck cruel and hard, and when it had finished its work, the man was no more.

The race of Adam is under death sentence. There is no commutation and no escape.

God cannot approve any of the fruits of sin, however innocent they may appear or beautiful to the eyes of men. God salvages the individual by liquidating him and then raising him again to newness of life.

That evangelism which draws friendly parallels between the ways of God and the ways of men is false to the Bible and cruel to the souls of its hearers. The faith of Christ does not parallel the world, it intersects it. In coming to Christ we do not bring our old life up onto a higher plane; we leave it at the cross. The corn of wheat must fall into the ground and die.

We who preach the gospel must not think of ourselves as public relations agents sent to establish good will between Christ and the world. We must not imagine ourselves commissioned to make Christ acceptable to big business, the press, the world of sports or modern education. We are not diplomats but prophets, and our message is not a compromise but an ultimatum.

God offers life, but not an improved old life. The life He offers is life out of death. It stands always on the far side of the cross. Whoever would possess it must pass under the rod. He must repudiate himself and concur in God's just sentence against him.

What does this mean to the individual, the condemned man who would find life in Christ Jesus? How can this theology be translated into life?

Simply, he must repent and believe. He must forsake his sins and then go on to forsake himself. Let him cover nothing, defend nothing, excuse nothing. Let him not seek to make terms with God, but let him bow his head before the stroke of God's stern displeasure and acknowledge himself worthy to die.

Having done this let him gaze with simple trust upon the risen Savior, and from Him will come life and rebirth and cleansing and power. The cross that ended the earthly life of Jesus now puts an end to the sinner; and the power that raised Christ from the dead now raises him to a new life along with Christ.

To any who may object to this or count it merely a narrow and private view of truth, let me say God has set His hallmark of approval upon this message from Paul's day to the present. Whether stated in these exact words or not, this has been the content of all preaching that has brought life and power to the world through the centuries. The mystics, the reformers, the revivalists have put their emphasis here, and signs and wonders and mighty operations of the Holy Ghost gave witness to God's approval.

Dare we, the heirs of such a legacy of power, tamper with the truth? Dare we with our stubby pencils erase the lines of the blueprint or alter the pattern shown us in the Mount? May God forbid. Let us preach the old cross and we will know the old power.

11. The Valley of Death

The Rending of the Veil

The interior journey of the soul from the wilds of sin into the enjoyed Presence of God is beautifully illustrated in the Old Testament tabernacle.

The returning sinner first entered the outer court where he offered a blood sacrifice on the brazen altar and washed himself in the laver that stood near it. Then through a veil he passed into the holy place where no natural light could come, but the golden candlestick which spoke of Jesus the Light of the World threw its soft glow over all. There also was the shewbread to tell of Jesus, the Bread of Life, and the altar of incense, a figure of unceasing prayer.

Though the worshipper had enjoyed so much, still he had not yet entered the Presence of God. Another veil separated from the Holy of Holies where above the mercy seat dwelt the very God Himself in awful and glorious manifestation. While the tabernacle stood, only the high priest could enter there, and that but once a year, with blood which he offered for his sins and the sins of the people.

It was this last veil which was rent when our Lord gave up the ghost on Calvary. The sacred writer explains that this rending of the veil opened the way for every worshipper in the world to come by the new and living way straight into the divine Presence.

Everything in the New Testament accords with this Old Testament picture. Ransomed men need no longer pause in fear to enter the Holy of Holies. *God wills that we should push on into His Presence and live our whole life there.* This is to be known to us in conscious experience. It is more than a doctrine to be held, it is a life to be enjoyed every moment of every day.

The greatest fact of the tabernacle was that *Jehovah was there*; a Presence was waiting within the veil. Similarly, the Presence of God is the central fact of Christianity. At the heart of the Christian message is God Himself waiting for His redeemed children to push in to conscious awareness of His Presence.

That type of Christianity which happens now to be the vogue knows this Presence only in theory. It fails to stress the Christian's privilege of present realization. According to its teachings we are in the Presence of God positionally, and nothing is said about the need to experience that Presence actually. The fiery urge that drove men like McCheyne is wholly missing.

And the present generation of Christians measures itself by this imperfect rule. Ignoble contentment takes the place of burning zeal. We are satisfied to rest in our judicial possessions, and for the most part we bother ourselves very little about the absence of personal experience.

Behind the veil is God, that God after Whom the world, with strange inconsistency, has felt, "if haply they might find Him." He has discovered Himself to some extent in nature, but more perfectly in the Incarnation; now He waits to show Himself in ravishing fulness to the humble of soul and the pure in heart.

The world is perishing for lack of the knowledge of God, and the Church is famishing for want of His Presence. The instant cure of most of our religious ills would be to enter the Presence in spiritual experience, to become suddenly aware that we are in God and that God is in us. This would lift us out of our pitiful narrowness and cause our hearts to be enlarged. This would burn away the impurities from our lives as the bugs and fungi were burned away by the fire that dwelt in the bush.

To penetrate, to push in sensitive living experience into the holy Presence, is a privilege open to every child of God. With the veil removed by the rending of Jesus' flesh, with nothing on God's side to prevent us from entering, why do we tarry without? Why do we consent to abide all our days just outside the Holy of Holies and never enter at all to look upon God?

We hear the Bridegroom say, "Let me see thy countenance, let me hear thy voice; for sweet is thy voice and thy countenance is comely." We sense that the call is for us, but still, we fail to draw near, and the years pass and we grow old and tired in the outer courts of the tabernacle. What doth hinder us?

The answer usually given, simply that we are "*cold,*" will not explain all the facts. There is something more serious than coldness of heart, something that may be back of that coldness and be the cause of its existence. What is it?

What but the presence of *a veil in our hearts*? A veil not taken away as the first veil was, but which remains there still, shutting out the light and hiding the face of God from us. It is the veil of our fleshly fallen nature living on, unjudged within us, uncrucified and unrepudiated. It is the close-woven veil of the self-life which we have never truly acknowledged, of which we have been secretly ashamed, and which for these reasons we have never brought to the judgment of the cross.

It is not too mysterious, this opaque veil, nor is it hard to identify. We have but to look in our own hearts and we shall see it there, sewn and patched and repaired it may be, but there nevertheless, an enemy to our lives and an effective block to our spiritual progress.

This veil is not a beautiful thing and it is not a thing about which we commonly care to talk, but I am addressing the thirsting souls who are determined to follow God, and I know they will not turn back because the way leads temporarily through the blackened hills. The urge of God within them will assure their continuing the pursuit. They will face the facts however unpleasant and endure the cross for the joy set before them. So I am bold to name the threads out of which this inner veil is woven.

It is woven of the fine threads of the self-life, the hyphenated sins of the human spirit. They are not something we do, they are something we *are*, and therein lies both their subtlety and their power.

To be specific, the self-sins are these: self-righteousness, self-pity, self-confidence, self-sufficiency, self-admiration, self-love and a host of others like them. They dwell too deep within us and are too much a part of our natures to come to our attention till the light of God is focused upon them. The grosser manifestations of these sins, egotism, exhibitionism, self-promotion, are strangely tolerated in Christian leaders even in circles of impeccable orthodoxy. They are so much in evidence as actually, for many people, to become identified with the gospel.

I trust it is not a cynical observation to say that they appear these days to be a requisite for popularity in some sections of the Church visible. Promoting self under the guise of promoting Christ is currently so common as to excite little notice.

One should suppose that proper instruction in the doctrines of man's depravity and the necessity for justification through the righteousness of Christ alone would deliver us from the power of the self-sins. But it does not work out that way.

Self can live unrebuked at the very altar. It can watch the bleeding Victim die and not be in the least affected by what it sees. It can fight for the faith of the Reformers and preach eloquently the creed of salvation by grace, and gain strength by its efforts. To tell all the truth, it seems actually to feed upon orthodoxy and is more at home in a Bible Conference than in a tavern. Our very state of longing after God may afford it an excellent condition under which to thrive and grow.

Self is the opaque veil that hides the Face of God from us. It can be removed only in spiritual experience, never by mere instruction. We might as well try to instruct leprosy out of our system. There must be a work of God in destruction before we are free. We must invite the cross to do its deadly work within us. We must bring our self-sins to the cross for judgment. We must prepare ourselves for an ordeal of suffering in some measure like that through which our Savior passed when He suffered under Pontius Pilate.

If the Spirit takes charge of your life, He will expect unquestioning obedience in everything. He will not tolerate in you the self-sins, even though they are permitted and excused by most Christians. You will find the Spirit to be in sharp opposition to the easy ways of the world and of the mixed multitude within the precincts of religion.

He will be jealous over you for good. He will take the direction of your life away from you. He will reserve the right to test you, to discipline you, to chasten you for your soul's sake. He may strip you of those borderline pleasures which other Christians enjoy but which are to you a source of refined evil.

Through it all He will enfold you in a love so vast, so mighty, so all-embracing, so wondrous that your very losses will seem like gains and your small pains like pleasures. Yet the flesh will whimper under His yoke and cry out against it as a burden too great to bear. And you will be permitted to enjoy the solemn privilege of suffering to *'fill up that which is behind of the afflictions of Christ'* in your flesh for His body's sake, which is the Church (Colossians 1:24).

If this appears severe, let us remember that the way of the cross is never easy. When we talk of the rending of the veil we are speaking in a figure, and the thought of it is poetical, almost pleasant; but in actuality there is nothing pleasant about it. In human experience that veil is made of living spiritual tissue; it is composed of the sentient, quivering stuff of which our whole beings consist, and to touch it is to touch us where we feel pain. To tear it away is to injure us, to hurt us and make us bleed. To say otherwise is to make the cross no cross and death no death at all.

It is never fun to die. To rip through the dear and tender stuff of which life is made can never be anything but deeply painful. Yet that is what the cross did to Jesus and it is what the cross would do to every man to set him free.

Before all who wish to follow Christ, the way lies clear. It is the way of death unto life. Always life stands just beyond death and beckons the man who is sick of himself to come and know the life more abundant. But to reach the new life he must pass through the valley of the shadow of death, and I know that at the sound of those words many will turn back and follow Christ no more. But *"to whom shall we go? Thou hast the words of eternal life."* (John 6:68)

Let us beware of tinkering with our inner life in hope of rending the veil ourselves. God must do everything for us. Our part is to yield and trust. We must confess, forsake, repudiate the self-life, and then reckon it crucified. But we must be careful to distinguish lazy "acceptance" from the real work of God. We must insist upon the work being done. We dare not rest content with a neat doctrine of self-crucifixion. That is to imitate Saul and spare the best of the sheep and the oxen.

When God calls a man to follow Him, He calls that man to follow Him regardless of the cost. The enemy can do his worst, but if a man is in God's hands, no harm can come to him. Nobody asked what it would cost a person to become a great football player. Or what it would cost a person to become a successful attorney. Or what it would cost a person to become a successful businessman. Everybody knows that the more important something is, the higher the cost. What costs you little or nothing is worth exactly that much. The challenge before us is simply this: What are we willing to pay, sacrifice or surrender in order to advance in living the crucified life?

Church history and Christian biography are filled with examples of what people have been willing to pay to live the crucified life. The martyrs of the Church form a long and glorious line. From the standpoint of the natural world, this sort of life does not look glamorous. But when we look at it from God's point of view, it takes on an altogether different perspective. The first Christian martyr was Stephen, who died at the feet of Saul, who later became the great apostle Paul. I am quite sure that Stephen's death made a great impression upon the young Saul.

Insist that the work be done in very truth and it will be done. The cross is rough, and it is deadly, but it is effective. It does not keep its victim hanging there forever. There comes a moment when its work is finished and the suffering victim dies. After that is resurrection glory and power, and the pain is forgotten for joy that the veil is taken away and we have entered in actual spiritual experience the Presence of the living God.

Resurrection Follows Crucifixion

It may be that there are some well-disposed followers who draw back because they cannot accept the morbidity which the idea of the cross seems to connote. They are lovers of the sun and find it too hard to think of living always in the shadows. They do not wish to dwell with death nor to live forever in an atmosphere of dying. Men crave life, but when they are told that life comes by the cross, they cannot understand how it can be, for they have learned to associate with the cross such typical images as memorial plaques, dim-lit aisles and ivy.

So they reject the true message of the cross, and with that message they reject the only hope of life known to the sons of man.

The truth is that God has never planned that His children should live forever stretched upon a cross. Christ Himself endured His cross for only six hours. When the cross had done its work life entered and took over. *"Wherefore God also hath highly exalted him, and given him a name which is above every name."* (Philippians 2:9)

His joyful resurrection followed hard upon His joyless crucifixion. But the first had to come before the second. The life that halts short of the cross is but a fugitive and condemned thing, doomed at last to be lost beyond recovery. That life which goes to the cross and loses itself there to rise again with Christ is a divine and deathless treasure. Death hath no more dominion over it. Whoever refuses to bring his old life to the cross is but trying to cheat death, and no matter how hard we may struggle against it, he is nevertheless fated to lose his life at last.

The man who takes his cross and follows Christ will soon find that his direction is *away* from the sepulcher. Death is behind him and a joyous and increasing life before. His days will be marked henceforth not by ecclesiastical gloom, the churchyard, the hollow tone, the black robe (which are all but the cerements of a dead church), but by *"joy unspeakable and full of glory."* (1 Peter 1:8)

Real faith must always mean more than passive acceptance. It dare not mean anything less than surrender of our doomed Adam-life to a merciful end upon the cross. That is, we won God's just sentence against our evil flesh and admit His right to end its unlovely career. We reckon ourselves to have been crucified with Christ and to have risen again to newness of life. Where such faith is, God will always work in line with our reckoning.

Then begins the divine conquest of our lives. This God accomplishes by an effective seizing upon, a sharp but love-impelled invasion of our natures. When He has overpowered our resistance, He binds us with the cords of love and draws us to Himself.

There, "faint with His loveliness" we lie conquered and thank God again and again for the blessed conquest. There, with moral sanity restored, we lift up our eyes and bless the Most High God. Then we go forth in faith to apprehend that for which we were first apprehended of God.

12. Worship and Fellowship

Work and Worship

To understand the relative importance of work and worship it is necessary to know the answer to the familiar question, "What is the chief end of man?" The answer given in the catechism, "To glorify God and to enjoy Him forever;" can scarcely be improved upon, though of course it is an outline only and needs to be enlarged somewhat if it is to be a full and satisfying answer.

The primary purpose of God in creation was to prepare moral beings spiritually and intellectually capable of worshiping Him. This has been so widely accepted by theologians and Bible expositors through the centuries that I shall make no attempt to prove it here. It is fully taught in the Scriptures and demonstrated abundantly in the lives of the saints. We may safely receive it as axiomatic and go on from there.

Once God existed in ineffable perfection of beauty with only the Persons of the Triune God to know and love each other.

"When heaven and earth were yet unmade,

When time was yet unknown,

Thou in Thy bliss and majesty Didst live and love alone."

Then God brought into being all things "that are in heaven, and that are in earth, visible and invisible, whether they be thrones, or dominions, or principalities, or powers: all things were created by him, and for him."

"How wonderful creation is.

The work that Thou didst bless,

God is the essence of all beauty, the fountain of all spiritual sweetness that can be known or desired by moral beings. He can and does love Himself with an unutterably holy love which we fallen creatures can gaze upon only with veiled faces and about which we dare speak only with hushed reverence and with humble admission of all but total ignorance.

By that moral disaster known in theology as the fall of man, an entire order of beings was wrenched violently loose from its proper place in the creational scheme and quite literally turned upside down. Human beings who had been specifically created to admire and adore the Deity turned away from Him and began to pour out their love, first upon themselves and then upon whatever cheap and tawdry objects their lusts and passions found.

The first chapter of Romans describes the journey of the human heart downward from the knowledge of God to the basest idolatry and fleshly sins. History is little more than the story of man's sin, and the daily newspaper a running commentary on it.

The work of Christ in redemption, for all its mystery, has a simple and understandable end: it is to restore men to the position from which they fell and bring them around again to be admirers and lovers of the Triune God. God saves men to make them worshipers.

This great central fact has been largely forgotten today, not by the liberals and the cults only, but by evangelical Christians as well. By direct teaching, by story, by example, by psychological pressure, we force our new converts to "go to work for the Lord." Ignoring the fact that God has redeemed them to make worshipers out of them, we thrust them out into "service," quite as if the Lord were recruiting laborers for a project instead of seeking to restore moral beings to a condition where they can glorify God and enjoy Him forever.

This is not to say that there is not work to be done. Most certainly there is, and God in His condescending love works in and through His redeemed children. Our Lord commands us to pray the Lord of the harvest that He will send forth laborers into His harvest field.

What we are overlooking is that no one can be a worker who is not first a worshiper. Labor that does not spring out of worship is futile and can only be wood, hay and stubble in the day that shall try every man's works.

It may be set down as an axiom that if we do not worship, we cannot work acceptably. The Holy Spirit can work through a worshiping heart and through no other kind. We may go through the motions and delude ourselves by our religious activity, but we are setting ourselves up for a shocking disillusionment some day.

Without doubt the emphasis in Christian teaching today should be on worship. There is little danger that we shall become merely worshipers and neglect the practical implications of the gospel. No one can long worship God in spirit and in truth before the obligation to holy service becomes too strong to resist. Fellowship with God leads straight to obedience and good works. That is the divine order and it can never be reversed.

Fellowship

One thing that instantly strikes the intelligent reader of the New Testament is the communal nature of the Christian faith. The social pronouns—we, they, us, them—are found everywhere. God's ideal is a fellowship of faith, a Christian community. He never intended that salvation should be received and enjoyed by the individual apart from the larger company of believers.

It is true that for each one there must be a personal encounter with God, and often that encounter takes place in the loneliness and silence of retirement. In that sacred moment there must be only God and the individual soul. The mysterious operation of God in regenerating grace and His further work of the Spirit's anointing are transactions so highly personal that no third party can know or understand what is taking place.

There are other experiences deep and wholly inward that cannot be shared with any other: Jacob at Bethel and Peniel, Moses at the burning bush, Christ in the garden, John in the Isle of Patmos are Bible examples, and Christian biography will reveal many more. A community of believers must be composed of persons who have each one met God in individual experience. No matter how large the family, each child must be born individually. Even twins or triplets are born one at a time. So it is in the local church. Each member must be born of the Spirit individually.

It will not escape the discerning reader that while each child is born separate from the rest it is born into a family, and after that must live in the fellowship of the rest of the household. And the man who comes to Christ in the loneliness of personal repentance and faith is also born into a family. The church is called the household of God, and it is the ideal place to rear young Christians.

Just as a child will not grow up to be a normal adult if forced to live alone, so the Christian who withdraws from the fellowship of other Christians will suffer great soul injury as a result. Such a one can never hope to develop normally. He'll get too much of himself and not enough of other people; and that is not good.

God has so created us that we need each other. We may and should go into our closet and pray to our heavenly Father in secret, but when the prayer is ended, we should go back to our people. That is where we belong.

To live within the religious family does not mean that we must approve everything that is done there. The prophets of Israel were often compelled to rebuke and warn their people, but they never left the bosom of Judaism. Even Christ went each Sabbath day and worshiped with the rest. The reformers and revivalists of post-Biblical times invariably lived close to the people. The loneliest and severest of them had their company of likeminded souls in which they found the help and consolation their grieving hearts required. Their example does not have the authority of revealed truth, but it does provide a rule we do well to follow.

No one is wise enough to live alone, nor good enough nor strong enough. God has made us to a large degree dependent upon each other. From our brethren we can learn how to do things and sometimes also we can learn how not to do them.

The best of singers must have a coach if he would avoid having his faults become chronic. The preacher who hears only himself preach will soon accept even his worst idiosyncrasies as marks of excellence. We need to listen to others that we may learn what to correct in ourselves.

This is true also of things moral and spiritual within the Christian family circle. A weak and faulty Christian, without his knowing it, can turn us from his way of life, and every holy and fruitful saint within our circle of fellowship becomes a goad to spur us onward toward a more perfect life.

Next to God Himself we need each other most. We are His sheep and it is our nature to live with the flock. And too, it might be well to remember that should we for a moment lose sight of the Shepherd we only have to go where His flock is to find Him again.

The Shepherd always stays with His flock.

13.Faith and Obedience

Centrality of Faith

The doctrine of faith is central in the divine scheme of salvation. God addresses His words to faith, and where no faith is, no true revelation is possible. "Without faith it is impossible to please him."

Every benefit flowing from the atonement of Christ comes to the individual through the gateway of faith. Forgiveness, cleansing, regeneration, the Holy Spirit, all answers to prayer, are given to faith and received by faith. There is no other way. This is common evangelical doctrine and is accepted wherever the cross of Christ is understood.

Because faith is so vital to all our hopes, so necessary to the fulfilment of every aspiration of our hearts, we dare take nothing for granted concerning it. Anything that carries with it so much of weal or woe, which indeed decides our heaven or our hell, is too important to neglect. We simply must not allow ourselves to be uninformed or misinformed. We must know.

For a number of years my heart has been troubled over the doctrine of faith as it is received and taught among evangelical Christians everywhere. Great emphasis is laid upon faith in orthodox circles, and that is good; but I am still troubled. Specifically, my fear is that the modern conception of faith is not the Biblical one; that when the teachers of our day use the word, they do not mean what Bible writers meant when they used it.

The causes of my uneasiness are these:

1. The lack of spiritual fruit in the lives of so many who claim to have faith.

2. The rarity of a radical change in the conduct and general outlook of persons professing their new faith in Christ as their personal Saviour.

3. The failure of our teachers to define or even describe the thing to

which the word faith is supposed to refer.

4. The heartbreaking failure of multitudes of seekers, be they ever so earnest, to make anything out of the doctrine or to receive any satisfying experience through it.

5. The real danger that a doctrine that is parroted so widely and received so uncritically by so many is false as understood by them.

6. I have seen faith put forward as a substitute for obedience, an escape from reality, a refuge from the necessity of hard thinking, a hiding place for weak character. I have known people to miscall by the name of faith high animal spirits, natural optimism, emotional thrills and nervous tics.

7. Plain horse sense ought to tell us that anything that makes no change in the man who professes it makes no difference to God either, and it is an easily observable fact that for countless numbers of persons the change from no-faith to faith makes no actual difference in the life.

Perhaps it will help us to know what faith is if we first notice what it is not. It is not the 'believing' of a statement we know to be true. The human mind is so constructed that it must of necessity believe when the evidence presented to it is convincing. It cannot help itself. When the evidence fails to convince, no faith is possible. No threats, no punishment, can compel the mind to believe against clear evidence.

Faith based upon reason is faith of a kind, it is true; but it is not of the character of Bible faith, for it follows the evidence infallibly and has nothing of a moral or spiritual nature in it.

Neither can the absence of faith based upon reason be held against anyone, for the evidence, not the individual, decides the verdict. To send a man to hell whose only crime was to follow evidence straight to its proper conclusion would be palpable injustice. To justify a sinner on the grounds that he had made up his mind according to the plain facts would be to make salvation the result of the workings of a common law of the mind as applicable to Judas as to Paul. It would take salvation out of the realm of the volitional and place it in the mental, where, according to the Scriptures, it surely does not belong.

True faith rests upon the character of God and asks no further proof than the moral perfections of the One who cannot lie. It is enough that God said it, and if the statement should contradict every one of the five senses and all the conclusions of logic as well, still the believer continues to believe. "Let God be true, but every man a liar," is the language of true faith. Heaven approves such faith because it rises above mere proofs and rests in the bosom of God.

In recent years among certain evangelicals there has arisen a movement designed to prove the truths of Scriptures by appeal to science. Evidence is sought in the natural world to support supernatural revelation. Snowflakes, blood, stones, strange marine creatures, birds and many other natural objects are brought forward as proof that the Bible is true. This is touted as being a great support to faith, the idea being that if a Bible doctrine can be proved to be true, faith will spring up and flourish as a consequence.

What these brethren do not see is that the very fact that they feel a necessity to seek proof for the truths of the Scriptures proves something else altogether, namely, their own basic unbelief. When God speaks unbelief asks, "How shall I know that this is true?" I AM THAT I AM is the only grounds for faith. To dig among the rocks or search under the sea for evidence to support the Scriptures is to insult the One who wrote them. I certainly do not believe that this is done intentionally; but I cannot see how we can escape the conclusion that it is done, nevertheless.

Faith as the Bible knows it is confidence in God and His Son Jesus Christ. It is the response of the soul to the divine character as revealed in the Scriptures; and even this response is impossible apart from the prior inworking of the Holy Spirit. Faith is a gift of God to a penitent soul and has nothing whatsoever to do with the senses or the data they afford. Faith is a miracle; it is the ability God gives to trust His Son. Anything that does not result in action in accord with the will of God is not faith but something else short of it.

Faith and morals are two sides of the same coin. Indeed, the very essence of faith is moral. Any professed faith in Christ as personal Savior that does not bring the life under plenary obedience to Christ as Lord is inadequate and must betray its victim at the last.

The man that believes will obey; failure to obey is convincing proof that there is not true faith present. To attempt the impossible God must give faith or there will be none, and He gives faith to the obedient heart only. Where real repentance is, there is obedience; for repentance is not only sorrow for past failures and sins, it is a determination to begin now to do the will of God as He reveals it to us.

Active Faith

A Christian is one who believes on Jesus Christ as Lord. With this statement every evangelical agrees. Indeed, there would appear to be nothing else to do, since the New Testament is crystal clear about the matter.

This first acknowledgment of Christ as Lord and Savior is usually followed by baptism and membership in a Protestant church, the one because it satisfies a craving for fellowship with others of like mind. A few Christians shy away from organized religion, but the vast majority, while they recognize the imperfections of the churches, nevertheless feel that they can serve their Lord better in the church than out of it.

There is, however, one serious flaw in all this. It is that many—would I overstate the case if I said the majority? —of those who confess their faith in Christ and enter into association with the community of believers have little joy in their hearts, no peace in their minds, and from all external appearances are no better morally than the ordinary educated citizen who takes no interest whatever in religion and, of course, makes no profession of Christianity. Why is this?

I believe it is the result of an inadequate concept of Christianity and an imperfect understanding of the revolutionary character of Christian discipleship.

There is nothing new in my conclusion. The evangelists are loud in their lamentation over the bodies of dead church members, as well they might be, and many thoughtful articles and books appear from time to time dealing with the serious hiatus between faith and practice among Christians.

Why then add another feeble voice to the many? Because many who lament the condition do not seem to know what to do about it, and because I believe that the way is plain, if hard, and that there is no excuse for going on at this poor dying rate when we can enjoy abundant life in Christ Jesus. True faith brings a spiritual and moral transformation and an inward witness that cannot be mistaken. These come when we stop believing in belief and start believing in the Lord Jesus Christ indeed.

True faith is not passive but active. It requires that we meet certain conditions, that we allow the teachings of Christ to dominate our total lives from the moment we believe.

The man of saving faith must be willing to be different from others. The effort to enjoy the benefits of redemption while enmeshed in the world is futile. We must choose one or the other; and faith quickly makes its choice, one from which there is no retreat.

The change experienced by a truly converted man is equal to that of a man moving to another country. The regenerated soul feels no more at home in the world than Abraham felt when he left Ur of the Chaldees and set out for the land of promise.

Apart from his own small company he was a stranger to everyone around him. He was called "Abraham the Hebrew," and if he spoke the language of the people among whom he took up his dwelling place, he spoke it with an accent. They all knew that he was not one of them.

This journey from Ur to Bethel is taken by every soul that sets out to follow Christ. It is, however, not a journey for the feet but for the heart. The newborn Christian is a migrant; he has come into the kingdom of God from his old home in the kingdom of man and he must get set for the violent changes that will inevitably follow.

One of the first changes will be a shift of interest from earth to heaven, from men to God, from time to eternity, from earthly gain to Christ and His eternal kingdom.

Suddenly, or slowly but surely, he will develop a new pattern of life. Old things will pass away and behold, all things will become new, first inwardly and then outwardly; for the change within him will soon begin to express itself by corresponding changes in his manner of living.

The transformation will show itself in many ways and his former friends will begin to worry about him. At first, they will tease him and then chide him. If he persists in his determination to follow Christ, they may begin to oppose and persecute.

The once-born never understand the twice-born, and still after thousands of years Cain hates Abel and Esau threatens Jacob. It is as true today as it was in Bible times that the man who hates his sins too much will get into trouble with those who do not hate sin enough. People resent having their friends turn away from them and by implication condemn their way of life.

The change will reveal itself further in what the new Christian reads, in the places he goes and the friends he cultivates, what he does with his time and how he spends his money. Indeed, faith leaves no area of the new believer's life unaffected.

The genuinely renewed man will have a new life center. He will experience a new orientation affecting his whole personality. He will become aware of a different philosophic outlook. Things he once held to be of value may suddenly lose all their attraction for him and he may even hate some things he formerly loved.

The man who recoils from this revolutionary kind of Christianity is retreating before the cross. But thousands do so retreat, and they try to make things right by seeking baptism and church membership. No wonder they are so dissatisfied.

Obeying the Scriptural Command to Love

One of the puzzling questions likely to turn up sooner or later to vex the seeking Christian is: how he can fulfil the scriptural command to love God with all his heart and his neighbor as himself.

The earnest Christian, as he meditates on his sacred obligation to love God and mankind, may experience a sense of frustration gendered by the knowledge that he just cannot seem to work up any emotional thrill over his Lord or his brothers. He wants to, but he cannot. The delightful wells of feeling simply will not flow.

Many honest persons have become discouraged by the absence of religious emotion and concluded that they are not really Christian after
all. They conclude that they must have missed the way somewhere
back there and their religion is little more than an empty profession.
So, they belabor themselves for their coldness for a while, and finally
settle into a state of dull discouragement, hardly knowing what to
think. They do believe in God; they do indeed trust Christ as their
Savior, but the love they hoped to feel consistently eludes them. What
is the trouble?

The problem is not a light one. A real difficulty is involved, one
which may be stated in the form of a question: How can I love by
commandment? Of all the emotions of which the soul is capable, love
is by far the freest, the most unreasoning, the one least likely to spring
up at the call of duty or obligation, and surely the one that will not
come at the command of another. No law has ever been passed that
can compel one moral being to love another, for by the very nature of
it love must be voluntary. No one can be coerced or frightened into
loving anyone. Love just does not come that way.

So what are we to do with our Lord's command to love God and our
neighbor?

To find our way out of the shadows and into the cheerful sunlight we
need only to know that there are two kinds of love: the love of feeling, and the love of willing. The one lies in the emotions, the other
in the will.

Over the one we may have little control. It comes and goes, rises and
falls, flares up and disappears as it chooses, and changes from hot to
warm to cool and back to warm again very much as does the weather.
Such love was not in the mind of Christ when He told His people to
love God and each other. We might as well command a butterfly to
light on our shoulder as to attempt to command this whimsical kind
of affection to visit our hearts.

The love the Bible enjoins is not the love of feeling; it is the love of
willing, the willed tendency of the heart. (For these two happy phrases I am indebted to another, a master of the inner life whose pen was
only a short time ago stilled by death.) God never intended that such

a being as man should be the plaything of his feelings. The emotional life is a proper and noble part of the total personality, but it is, by its very nature, of secondary importance. Religion lies in the will, and so does righteousness. The only good that God recognizes is a willed good; the only valid holiness is a willed holiness.

The will is the automatic pilot that keeps the soul on course. "Flying is easy," said a friend who flies his own plane. "Just take her up, point her in the direction you want her to go and set the pilot. After that she will fly herself." While we must not press the figure too far, it is yet blessedly true that the will, not the feelings, determines moral direction.

The root of all evil in human nature is the corruption of the will. The thoughts and intents of the heart are wrong, and as a consequence the whole life is wrong.

It should be a cheering thought that before God every man is what he wills to be. The first requirement in conversion is a rectified will. "If any man will," says our Lord, and leaves it there. To meet the requirements of love toward God the soul need but will to love and the miracle begins to blossom like the budding of Aaron's rod.

14.Repentance and the Will

What Repentance Involves

Repentance is primarily a change of moral purpose, a sudden and often violent reversal of the soul's direction. The prodigal son took his first step upward from the pigsty when he said, *"I will arise and go to my father."* As he had once willed to leave his father's house, now he willed to return. His subsequent action proved his expressed purpose to be sincere. He did return.

Someone may infer from the above that we are ruling out the joy of the Lord as a valid part of the Christian life. While no one who reads these columns regularly would be likely to draw such an erroneous conclusion, a chance reader might be led astray; a further word of explanation is therefore indicated.

It is the profound conviction that we are wholly unworthy of future blessedness, that we are indeed by nature fitted only for destruction, that leads to true repentance. The man who inwardly believes that he is too good to perish will certainly perish, unless he experiences a radical change of heart about himself.

To love God with all our heart we must first of all will to do so. We should repent our lack of love and determine from this moment on to make God the object of our devotion. We should set our affections on things above and aim our hearts toward Christ and heavenly things. We should read the Scriptures devotionally every day and prayerfully obey them, always firmly willing to love God with all our heart and our neighbor as ourself.

If we do these things, we may be sure that we shall experience a wonderful change in our whole inward life. We shall soon find to our great delight that our feelings are becoming less erratic and are beginning to move in the direction of the "willed tendency of the heart."

Our emotions will become disciplined and directed. We shall begin to taste the "piercing sweetness" of the love of Christ. Our religious affection will begin to mount evenly on steady wings instead of flitting about idly without purpose or intelligent direction. The whole life, like a delicate instrument, will be tuned to sing the praises of Him who loved us and washed us from our sins in His own blood.

But first of all, we must will, for the will is master of the heart.

I've heard for the last thirty years that repentance is a change of mind, and I believe it, of course, as far as it goes. But that's just what's the matter with us. We have reduced repentance to a change of mind. It is a mental act, indeed, but I point out that repentance is not likely to do us much good until it ceases to be a change of mind only and becomes a wound within our spirit.

No man has truly repented until his sin has wounded him near to death, until the wound has broken him and defeated him and taken all the fight and self-assurance out of him, and he sees himself as the one who nailed his Savior on the tree.

I don't know about you, but the only way I can keep right with God is to keep contrite, to keep a sense of contrition upon my spirit. Now there's a lot of cheap and easy getting rid of sin and getting your repentance disposed of. But the great Christians, in and out of the Bible, have been those who were wounded with a sense of contrition so deeply that they never quite got over the thought and the feeling that they personally had crucified Jesus.

The great Bishop Usher each week used to go down by the riverbank and there all Saturday afternoon kneel by a log and bewail his sins before his God. Perhaps that was the secret of his greatness.

Let us beware of vain and over-hasty repentance, and particularly let us beware of no repentance at all. We are a sinful race, ladies and gentlemen, a sinful people, and until the knowledge has hit hard, until it has wounded us, until it has got through and past the little department of our theology, it has done us no good. A man can believe in total depravity and never have any sense of it for himself at all. Lots of us believe in total depravity who have never been wounded with the knowledge that we've sinned.

Repentance is a wound I pray we may all feel.

Truth, Feeling, and Act

Emotion, says Drever's *Dictionary of Psychology*, is a state of excitement or perturbation, marked by strong feeling and usually an impulse toward a definite form of behavior.

"Excitement, perturbation, feeling." These are states of mind we are all familiar with. In a world as violent and full of conflict as this, these come and go, blaze up and die down in the average man's bosom a hundred times a day. The normal man and woman will in the course of a few months experience every degree of emotion from near ecstasy to mild dejection without apparently being any the better or the worse for it.

Of course, I have in mind here only the normal man and woman. The psychopathic personality lies outside the field of this study.

The emotions are neither to be feared nor despised, for they are a normal part of us as God made us in the first place. Indeed, the full human life would be impossible without them. One recoils from the thought of the man who lacked all feeling. He would be either a cold, naked intellect, such as inhabits the pages of the science fiction novel, or a mere vegetable, such as is sometimes found in the incurable wards of our mental hospitals.

The right relation of intellect to feeling and feeling to will is disclosed in Matthew 14:14. "*And Jesus went forth, and saw a great multitude, and was moved with compassion toward them, and he healed their sick.*"

Intellectual knowledge of the suffering of the people stirred His pity and His pity moved Him to heal them. This is how it was with the ideal Man whose total organism was perfectly adjusted to itself; and this is the way it is with us in a less perfect measure.

A state of emotion always comes between the knowledge and the act. A feeling of pity would never arise in the human breast unless aroused by a mental picture of others' distress, and without the emotional bump to set off the will there would be no act of mercy. That is the way we are constituted. Whether the emotion aroused by a mental picture be pity, love, fear, desire, grief, there can be no act of the will without it.

What I am saying here is nothing new. Every mother, every states-man, every leader of men, every preacher of the Word of God knows that a mental picture must be presented to the listener before he can be moved to act, even though it be for his own advantage.

God intended that truth should move us to moral action. The mind receives ideas, mental pictures of things as they are. These excite the feelings, and these in turn move the will to act in accordance with the truth. That is the way it should be, and would be had not sin entered and wrought injury to our inner life.

Because of sin the simple sequence of *truth—feeling—action* may break down in any of its three parts. The mind which is created to receive truth is often turned over to falsehood, and the feelings thus aroused may incite the will to evil action. The contemplation of any wrong or forbidden thing cannot but inflame the feelings to sympathy with evil.

A regrettable example of this was David's long gaze at the beautiful Bathsheba in the act of bathing. The king was moved by what he saw and acted accordingly, and the bitter and tragic consequences dogged him to the end of his days.

He saw, he felt, he acted, precisely as his Lord did centuries later when He healed the sick. The difference in the moral quality of the acts of the two men resulted from the difference in their feelings, and these were the result of the objects that aroused the feelings. David saw a beautiful woman; Christ saw a suffering multitude. One gaze led to sin, the other to an act of mercy; but both followed the simple law of their inner structure.

Another breakdown in the truth—feeling—act sequence comes when the heart for selfish reasons deliberately hardens itself against the Word of God. This is the state of all who love darkness rather than light, and for that reason either withdraw from the light altogether or, when exposed to it, stubbornly refuse to obey it.

The covetous man looks on human need and sternly refuses to be moved by it. To yield to the impulse of generosity naturally aroused by the sight of poverty would require him to give up some of his cherished hoard, and this he will not do. So, the fountain of generosity is frozen at its source. The miser keeps his gold, the poor man suffers on in his poverty, and the whole course of nature is upset. Is it any wonder that God hates covetousness?

But be sure that human feelings can never be completely stifled. If they are forbidden their normal course, like a river they will cut another channel through the life and flow out to curse and ruin and destroy.

The Christian who gazes too long on the carnal pleasures of this world cannot escape a certain feeling of sympathy with them, and that feeling will inevitably lead to behavior that is worldly. And to expose our hearts to truth and consistently refuse or neglect to obey the impulses it arouses is to stymie the motions of life within us and, if persisted in, to grieve the Holy Spirit into silence.

Scripture and our own human constitution agree to teach us to love truth and to obey the sweet impulses of righteousness it raises within us. If we love our own soul, we dare do nothing else.

Choose to Obey or not

The whole matter of moral choice centers around Jesus Christ. Christ stated it plainly: "*He that is not with me is against me*," and "*No man cometh unto the Father, but by me.*"

The gospel message embodies three distinct elements: an announcement, a command, and a call. It announces the good news of redemption accomplished in mercy; it commands all men everywhere to repent; and it calls all men to surrender to the terms of grace by believing on Jesus Christ as Lord and Savior.

We must all choose whether we will obey the gospel or turn away in unbelief and reject its authority. Our choice is our own, but the consequences of the choice have already been determined by the sovereign will of God, and from this there is no appeal.

15.Prayer and Obedience

God Answers the Prayers of the Obedient

Contrary to popular opinion, the cultivation of a psychology of un-critical belief is not an unqualified good, and if carried too far it may be a positive evil. The whole world has been booby-trapped by the devil, and the deadliest trap of all is the religious one. Error never looks so innocent as when it is found in the sanctuary.

One field where harmless-looking but deadly traps appear in great profusion is the field of prayer. There are more sweet notions about prayer than could be contained in a large book, all of them wrong and all highly injurious to the souls of men.

I think of one such false notion that is found often in pleasant places consorting smilingly with other notions of unquestionable orthodoxy. It is that God always answers prayer.

This error appears among the saints as a kind of all-purpose philo-sophic therapy to prevent any disappointed Christian from suffering too great a shock when it becomes evident to him that his prayer expectations are not being fulfilled. It is explained that God always answers prayer, either by saying *Yes* or by saying *No*, or by substitut-ing something else for the desired favor.

Now, it would be hard to invent a neater trick than this to save face for the petitioner whose requests have been rejected for non-obedience. Thus, when a prayer is not answered he has but to smile brightly and explain, "God said No." It is all so very comfortable. His wobbly faith is saved from confusion and his conscience is permitted to lie undisturbed. But I wonder if it is honest.

To receive an answer to prayer as the Bible uses the term and as Christians have understood it historically, two elements must be pres-ent:

(1) A clear-cut request made to God for a specific favor, and

(2) a clear-cut granting of that favor by God in answer to the request.

There must be no semantic twisting, no changing of labels, no altering of the map during the journey to help the embarrassed tourist to find himself.

When we go to God with a request that He modify the existing situation for us, that is, that He answer prayer, there are two conditions that we must meet:

(1) We must pray in the will of God, and

(2) we must be on what old-fashioned Christians often call "praying ground"; that is, we must be living lives pleasing to God.

It is futile to beg God to act contrary to His revealed purposes. To pray with confidence, the petitioner must be certain that his request falls within the broad will of God for His people.

The second condition is also vitally important. God has not placed Himself under obligation to honor the requests of worldly, carnal or disobedient Christians. He hears and answers the prayers only of those who walk in His way.

"Beloved, if our heart condemn us not, then have we confidence toward God. And whatsoever we ask, we receive of him, because we keep his commandments, and do those things that are pleasing in his sight ... If ye abide in me, and my words abide in you, ye shall ask what ye will, and it shall be done unto you." (1 John 3:21-22; John 15:7)

God wants us to pray and He wants to answer our prayers, but He makes our use of prayer as a privilege to commingle with His use of prayer as a discipline. To receive answers to prayer we must meet God's terms. If we neglect His commandments, our petitions will not be honored. He will alter situations only at the request of obedient and humble souls.

The God-always-answers-prayer sophistry leaves the praying man without discipline. By the exercise of this bit of smooth casuistry he ignores the necessity to live soberly, righteously and godly in this present world, and actually takes God's flat refusal to answer his prayer as the very answer itself.

Of course, such a man will not grow in holiness; he will never learn how to wrestle and wait; he will never know correction; he will not hear the voice of God calling him forward; he will never arrive at the place where he is morally and spiritually fit to have his prayers answered. His wrong philosophy has ruined him.

That is why I turn aside to expose the bit of bad theology upon which his bad philosophy is founded. The man who accepts it never knows where he stands. He never knows whether or not he has true faith, for if his request is not granted, he avoids the implication by the simple dodge of declaring that God switched the whole thing around and gave him something else. He will not allow himself to shoot at a target, so he cannot tell how good or how bad a marksman he is.

Of certain persons James says plainly: "*Ye ask, and receive not, because ye ask amiss, that ye may consume it upon your lusts.*" From that brief sentence we may learn that God refuses some requests because they who make them are not morally worthy to receive the answer.

But this means nothing to the one who has been seduced into the belief that God always answers prayer. When such a man asks and receives not, he passes his hand over the hat and comes up with the answer in some other form. One thing he clings to with great tenacity: God never turns anyone away, but invariably grants every request.

The truth is that God always answers the prayer that accords with His will as revealed in the Scriptures, provided the one who prays is obedient and trustful. Further than this we dare not go.

Prayers of the Carnal

Of all forms of deception, self-deception is the deadliest, and of all deceived persons the self-deceived are the least likely to discover the fraud.

The reason for this is simple. When a man is deceived by another he is deceived against his will. He is contending against an adversary and is temporarily the victim of the other's guile. Since he expects his foe to take advantage of him, he is watchful and quick to suspect trickery. Under such circumstances it is possible to be deceived sometimes and for a short while, but because the victim is resisting, he may break out of the trap and escape before too long.

With the self-deceived it is quite different. He is his own enemy and is working a fraud upon himself. He wants to believe the lie and is psychologically conditioned to do so.

He does not resist the deceit but collaborates with it against himself. There is no struggle, because the victim surrenders before the fight begins. He enjoys being deceived.

It is altogether possible to practice fraud upon our own souls and go deceived to judgment. "*If a man think himself to be something, when he is nothing,*" said Paul, "*he deceiveth himself.*" With this agrees the inspired James: "*If any man among you seem to be religious, and bridleth not his tongue, but deceiveth his own heart, this man's religion is vain.*"

The farther we push into the sanctuary, the greater becomes the danger of self-deception. The deeply religious man is far more vulnerable than the easygoing fellow who takes his religion lightly. This latter may be deceived, but he is not likely to be self-deceived.

Under the pressure of deep spiritual concern, and before his heart has been wholly conquered by the Spirit of God, a man may be driven to try every dodge to save face and preserve a semblance of his old independence. This is always dangerous and if persisted in may prove calamitous.

The fallen heart is by nature idolatrous. There appears to be no limit to which some of us will go to save our idol, while at the same time telling ourselves eagerly that we are trusting in Christ alone. It takes a violent act of renunciation to deliver us from the hidden idol, and since very few modern Christians understand that such an act is necessary, and only a small number of those who know are willing to do, it follows that relatively few professors of the Christian faith these days have ever experienced the painful act of renunciation that frees the heart from idolatry.

Prayer is usually recommended as the panacea for all ills and the key to open every prison door, and it would indeed be difficult to overstate the advantages and privilege of Spirit-inspired prayer. But we must not forget that unless we are wise and watchful, prayer itself may become a source of self-deception. There are as many kinds of prayer as there are problems, and some kinds are not acceptable to God.

The prophets of the Old Testament denounced Israel for trying to hide their iniquities behind their prayers. Christ flatly rejected the prayers of hypocrites and James declared that some religious persons ask and receive not because they ask amiss.

To escape self-deception the praying man must come out clean and honest. He cannot hide in the cross while concealing in his bosom the golden wedge and the goodly Babylonish garment. Grace will save a man but it will not save him and his idol. The blood of Christ will shield the penitent sinner alone, but never the sinner and his idol. Faith will justify the sinner, but it will never justify the sinner and his sin.

No amount of pleading will make evil good or wrong right. A man may engage in a great deal of humble talk before God and get no response because unknown to himself he is using prayer to disguise disobedience. He may lie for hours in sackcloth and ashes with no higher motive than to try to persuade God to come over on his side so he can have his own way. He may grovel before God in a welter of self-accusation, refuse to give up his secret sin and be rejected for his pains. It can happen.

Dr. H. M. Shuman once said to me in private conversation that he believed the one quality God required a man to have before He would save him was honesty. With this I heartily agree. However dishonest the man may have been before, he must put away his duplicity if he is to be accepted before the Lord. Double dealing is unutterably offensive to God. The insincere man has no claim on mercy. For such a man the cross of Christ provides no remedy. Christ can and will save a man who has been dishonest, but He cannot save him while he is dishonest. Absolute candor is an indispensable requisite to salvation.

How may we remain free from self-deception? The answer sounds old-fashioned and dull but here it is: Mean what you say and nev-

Yet one of the most effective talking points that popular Christianity has is the idea that God exists to help people to get ahead in this world. The God of the poor has become the God of an affluent society. Christ no longer refuses to be a judge or a divider between money-hungry brothers. He can now be persuaded to assist the brother that has accepted Him to get the better of the brother who has not.

A crass example of the modern effort to use God for selfish purposes is the well-known comedian who, after repeated failures, made a promise to someone he called God. If He would help him to make good in the entertainment world, he would repay Him by giving generously to the care of sick children. Shortly afterward he hit the big time in the night clubs and on television. He has kept his word and is raising large sums of money to build children's hospitals. These contributions to charity, he feels, are a small price to pay for a success in one of the sleaziest fields of human endeavor.

One might excuse the act of this entertainer as something to be expected of a twentieth century pagan. But the fact that multitudes of evangelicals in North America should actually believe that God had anything to do with the whole business is not so easily overlooked. This low and false view of Deity is one major reason for the immense popularity God enjoys these days among well-fed Westerners.

The teaching of the Bible is that God is Himself the end for which man was created. *"Whom have I in heaven but thee?"* cried the psalmist, *"and there is none upon earth that I desire beside thee."* (Psalm 73:25)

The first and greatest commandment is to love God with every power of our entire being. Where love like that exists, there can be no place for a second object. If we love God as much as we should, we surely cannot dream of a loved object beyond Him which He might help us to obtain.

Bernard of Clairvaux begins his radiant little treatise on the love of God with a question and an answer.

The question: *why should we love God?* The answer: *because He is God.*

He develops the idea further, but for the enlightened heart little more need be said. We should love God because He is God. Beyond this the angels cannot think.

Being who He is, God is to be loved for His own sake. *He* is the reason for our loving Him, just as *He* is the reason for His loving us, and for every other act He has performed, is performing, and will perform world without end.

God's primary reason for everything is His own good pleasure. The search for secondary reasons is gratuitous and mostly futile. It affords occupation for theologians and adds pages to books on doctrine, but that it ever turns up any true explanations is doubtful.

But it is the nature of God to share. His mighty acts of creation and redemption were done for His good pleasure, but His pleasure extends to all created things. One has but to look at a healthy child at play or listen to the song of a bird at sundown and he will know that God meant His universe to be a joyful one.

Those who have been spiritually enabled to love God for Himself will find a thousand fountains springing up from the rainbow-circled Throne and bringing countless treasures. These are to be received with reverent thanksgiving as being the overflow of God's love for His children. Each gift is a bonus of grace which, because it was not sought for itself, may be enjoyed without injury to the soul. These include the simple blessings of life, such as health, a home, a family, congenial friends, food, shelter, the pure joys of nature or the more artificial pleasures of music and art.

The effort to find these treasures by direct search apart from God has been the major activity of mankind through the centuries; and this has been man's burden and man's woe. The effort to gain them as the ulterior motive back of accepting Christ may be something new under the sun; but new or old it is an evil that can only bring judgment at last.

God wills that we should love Him for Himself alone with no hidden reasons, trusting Him to be to us all our natures require. Our Lord said all this much better: "*Seek ye first the kingdom of God, and his righteousness; and all these things shall be added unto you.*" (Matthew 6:33)

16. Why The Holy Spirit?

Our Lord told His disciples they had a huge job before them: to preach the gospel to every creature, to go everywhere throughout the world and tell them that they could be saved by faith in Jesus Christ. Yet He forbade them to go immediately. He said, "You are to go," and when they started, He said, "Now, don't go." There must have been a compelling reason for His telling them to wait.

Christ outlined for them a program of world evangelization and told them in Acts, "*But ye shall receive power, after that the Holy Ghost is come upon you: and ye shall be witnesses unto me both in Jerusalem, and in all Judaea, and in Samaria, and unto the uttermost part of the earth.*" (Acts 1:8)

He said they were to enter a new era. God was to introduce a change of dispensation, but He was not to introduce a change of dispensation apart from a stepped up and elevated spiritual experience. It was not only to be a change over from one dispensation to another. It was to be introduced by a coming down of a new afflatus from above. Something was to come that had not been there before. And it was to enter them and possess them. It was to bring God to them in a way He was not with them then, and was to enter them and dwell there.

That is the difference between Christianity and all of the oriental cults and occult religions. The occult religions try to wake up what you already have. Christianity says, what you have isn't enough; I'm going to send an enduement from above that shall enter you and be to you what you lack. There is the difference.

They say, "Wake up your solar plexus," which is one religion. I do not even know where mine is. I could not even locate the thing. Then they say, "Stir up the thing that is in you." What is the use?

If there were four or five lions coming, you could not say to a little French poodle, "Wake up the lion in you." That would not work. They would chew the poor little fellow up and swallow him, haircut and all, because a French poodle just is not sufficient for the lion. If God wanted a French poodle to fight a lion, He would have to put the heart and body of the lion in the poodle. He would have to make him bigger and stronger than his opponent.

That is exactly what the Holy Spirit says He does. The simple fact is creative powers do not lie in us. We begin to die the moment we are born.

You and I do not have hidden potentials, creative impulses, and all that kind of stuff in us. We walk around on the earth barely able to keep going. As we get older, the gravitational pull slowly drags us down and humps us over. Finally, we give up one day with a sigh and go back to Mother Earth. That is the kind of potential we have. We have the potential to be a corpse.

God Almighty says, "I do not want to wake up the power that lies in you. Ye shall receive the power of the Holy Spirit coming upon you." That is a different thing altogether, my friend.

If we only need to be awakened, the Lord would simply have gone around waking us up. But we needed more than just to be awakened. We need to be endued with power from on high.

What was the Difference

They were to enter a new era and it was to mark something grandly new and an enriched spiritual condition. What difference did this make? What difference did it make to these disciples?

Consciousness of God's Presence

The first is a sudden brilliant consciousness of God being actually present. They had this. They knew Jesus and loved Jesus; but now, when the Holy Spirit came upon them, they had a sudden consciousness; brilliant consciousness of God being actually present. A veil was raised and they felt God. A sense of acute God-consciousness was on them from that time on. They knew themselves to be in immediate contact with another world.

My brethren, that is exactly what the average Gospel church does not have today. We are not in contact with another world. We are very happily in contact with this world. But those disciples were other-worldly. Many liberals have made fun of that hyphenated expression "other-worldly." They say, "You are so everlastingly good you are no good. You are so heavenly you are no good on earth."

I can tell you that only the Holy Spirit can give, bring, impart and maintain that sense of the divine presence.

The Joy of the Holy Spirit

The second difference the Holy Spirit made was He gave them the joy of the Holy Ghost. That is, a change of emotional tone came at once.

I am thinking about God's dear people always praying for joy and praying for light and praying for every benediction, and yet they do not get it. They want to pray for it Sunday all day long and then Sunday night go home and sigh, and go to bed and give up, and come back and do the same thing over again.

We ought to know better. Christians work themselves up Sunday, then go back down, and start all over on a lower level on Monday. Perhaps they work themselves up a little on Wednesday night, but the point is, it never seems to stick. The bell loses its clapper. It does not ring any more.

The happiness of these disciples was the happiness of the Holy Ghost. God sang, and the Scripture says that we are to be filled with the Spirit singing. Singing and making melody in your hearts unto the Lord. Choirs ought not to sing for churches, they ought to sing for the Lord and let the church hear. That is the way it is when the Holy Ghost is in control. We are to be filled with the Holy Ghost, singing unto the Lord, and the people hear. Then they are blessed while we sing unto the Lord.

Penetrating Power of Words

There was the joy of the Holy Ghost and there is the third, the power of their words to penetrate and arrest. I do not have to tell you there is a difference between the penetrating power of words. Even the same words and the same sentence spoken by one man will put you under conviction, spoken by another man leaves you completely cold. The Holy Spirit makes that difference. He said, "Ye shall be endued with power," and the word power there means the ability to do.

When Peter preached at Pentecost, they were stricken in their hearts when they heard him. They were pierced, stricken through in their hearts and they said, "Men and brethren, what shall we do?"

If you will look at the second chapter of Acts, you will see what it says there. They were pricked in their hearts and said unto Peter, "Men and brethren, what shall we do?"

The Holy Spirited penetrated, and that is one of the works of the Holy Spirit. He comes and penetrates; He sharpens the point of the arrows of the man of God.

Authority

They had, fourth, a clear sense of the reality of everything. You noticed that in the Four Gospels, they were asking questions and in the book of Acts, they were answering questions. That is the difference. That is the difference between a Spirit-filled man and one that is not. The man of God, the preacher that is not Spirit-filled makes a great deal, and one of his phrases is likely to be "and now let us ask ourselves this question." Have you ever heard this from the pulpit? I have often wondered why the reverend wanted to ask himself a question. Why didn't he settle that at home before he came to church? Always asking questions. "And, now, what shall we say?"

But when they got to the book of Acts, they began to answer questions. And they stood with authority. The same Peter that sneaked around, warmed his hand at the world's fire, and lied to the little woman that recognized his accent. He was standing boldly to preach the word of the Lord. That was the difference. There was authority there. That is our trouble.

I know there ought to be a lot more authority in the pulpit than there is. A preacher ought to reign from the pulpit as a king from his throne. Not by law, not by regulations, or not by board meetings and annual meetings only, although I believe in them too. He ought to by moral ascendancy. When a man of God stands to speak, he ought to have the authority of God on him so he makes the people responsible to listen to him. When they do not listen to him, they are accountable to God for turning down the divine word.

Instead of that, we have a lot of tabby-cats with their claws carefully trimmed in the seminary. They can paw over their congregations and never scratch them at all. They have had their claws trimmed. They are just as soft and sweet.

I believe in the authority of God. And I believe if a man does not have it, he ought to go away somewhere and wait until he gets the authority. Then stand up to speak if he has to begin by preaching on a soapbox on a street corner or go to a rescue mission and preach with authority. They had it in those days. When they stood up, there was authority there.

Separation From the World

Then, a sharp separation between them and the world. I suppose I ought to skip that. On their part, they were seeing another world. They were looking at another world. They really saw another world. Nowadays, evangelical Christianity is trying to convert this world to the Church. Bringing it in, head over heels, world and all. Unregenerated, uncleansed, unshriven, unbaptized, unsanctified ... bringing the world right into the church.

If you can just get a big-shot to say something nice about the church, they rush into print, usually in bad English, and tell about this fellow. What nice things he said. I do not give a hoot about big-shots because I serve a living Savior and Jesus Christ is Lord of lords and King of kings. He picked up a farm boy from the hills of Pennsylvania, anointed my head with oil and said, "Go out and tell them."

And I have been telling them. I do not care whether people listen, but they will know a prophet has been among them. I believe every man ought to have this authority, this separation, that will make him see another world. If there is any converting, it is going to be a one-way street. The world is going to come to us; we are not going to the world.

Delight in Prayer

Then another thing; they took a great delight in prayer. The only one who could stay awake praying in the Gospels was Jesus. Others tried to pray but they came to Him and said, "Teach us to pray." But He knew you could not teach anybody to pray.

They are giving courses on how to pray, today. How ridiculous. It is like giving a course on how to fall in love. No, when the Holy Spirit comes, He takes the things of God and translates them into language our hearts understand. Even if we do not know the will of God, the Holy Ghost does, and He prays with groanings that cannot be uttered. These disciples were praying people. They were always praying somewhere, always off somewhere praying. Before that, they would fall asleep. Now, nobody was sleeping. They had a great delight in prayer.

Love for Scripture

And a passionate love for the Scriptures. This is the seventh thought. Did you know that Jesus quoted the Scriptures in the Gospels but the disciples quoted the Scriptures in the Acts? There was the difference.

I remember a dear saint of God who said once, years ago, "When I was filled with the Spirit, I loved the Scriptures so much that if I could have gotten more of the word inside me by eating it, I would have eaten the book, leather and everything, if I could have gotten more of the book inside my heart."

The word of God is sweet to the Spirit-filled person because the Spirit wrote the Scriptures. You cannot read the Scriptures with the spirit of Adam, for the Spirit of God inspired them. The spirit of the world does not appreciate the Scriptures. It is the Spirit of God that appreciates the Scriptures.

One little flash of the Holy Ghost will give you more inward divine illumination on the meaning of the text then all the commentators that ever commentated. Yet I have commentaries. I am not talking against things. I am only trying to show you that if you have everything and have not the fullness of the Holy Ghost, you are nothing. When you have the Holy Spirit, then God may use anything and everything. He uses boards and ladies praying groups and commentators and all the rest.

But we try to get along without the Holy Spirit and that is the terrible thing. How different it is today, the contrast. We live by hearsay. A vague sense of reality and wonder is missing.

We may go astray by assuming that we can do spiritual work without spiritual power. I have heard the notion seriously advanced that whereas once to win men to Christ it was necessary to have a gift from the Holy Spirit, now religious movies make it possible for anyone to win souls, without such spiritual anointing! "Whom the gods would destroy they first make mad." Surely such a notion is madness, but until now I have not heard it challenged among the evangelicals.

David Brainerd once compared a man without the power of the Spirit trying to do spiritual work to a workman without fingers attempting to do manual labor. The figure is striking but it does not overstate the facts. The Holy Spirit is not a luxury meant to make deluxe Christians, as an illuminated frontispiece and a leather binding make a deluxe book. The Spirit is an imperative necessity. Only the Eternal Spirit can do eternal deeds.

17.The Holy Spirit as the Cure

Merging of Wills

The deep disease of the human heart is a will broken loose from its center, like a planet which has left its central sun and started to revolve around some strange body from outer space which may have moved in close enough to draw it away. When Satan said, "I will," he broke loose from his normal center, and the disease with which he has infected the human race is the disease of disobedience and revolt. Any adequate scheme of redemption must take into account this revolt and must undertake to restore again the human will to its proper place in the will of God.

In accord with this underlying need for the healing of the will, the Holy Spirit, when He effects His gracious invasion of the believing heart, must win that heart to glad and voluntary obedience to the whole will of God. The cure must be wrought from within; no outward conformity will do. Until the will is sanctified, the man is still a rebel, just as an outlaw is still an outlaw at heart even though he may be yielding grudging obedience to the sheriff who is taking him to prison.

The Holy Spirit achieves this inward cure by merging the will of the redeemed man with His own. This is not accomplished at one stroke. There must be, it is true, some kind of overall surrender of the will to Christ before any work of grace can be done. But the full merging of every part of life with the life of God in the Spirit is likely to be a longer process than we in our creature impatience would wish.

The most advanced soul may be shocked and chagrined to discover some private area within his life where he had been, unknown to himself, acting as lord and proprietor of that which he thought he had given to God. It is the work of the in-living Spirit to point out these moral discrepancies and correct them. He does not, as is sometimes said, "break" the human will, but He does invade it and bring it gently to a joyous union with the will of God.

To will the will of God is to do more than give unprotesting consent to it; it is rather to choose God's will with positive determination. As the work of God advances, the Christian finds himself free to choose whatever he will, and he gladly chooses the will of God as his highest conceivable good.

Such a man has found life's highest goal. He has been placed beyond the little disappointments that plague the rest of men. Whatever happens to him is the will of God for him and that is just what he most ardently desires.

But it is only fair to state that this condition is one not reached by many of the busy Christians of our busy times. Until it is reached, however, the Christian's peace cannot be complete. There must be still a certain inward controversy, a sense of spiritual disquiet which poisons our joy and greatly reduces our power.

Conditions for Filling

For all God's good will toward us, He is unable to grant us our heart's desires till all our desires have been reduced to one. When we have dealt with our carnal ambitions, when we have trodden upon the lion and adder of the flesh, have trampled the dragon of self-love under our feet, and have truly reckoned ourselves to have died unto sin—then and only then can God raise us to newness of life and fill us with His blessed Holy Spirit.

It is easy to learn the doctrine of personal revival and victorious living. It is quite another thing to take our cross and plod on to the dark and bitter hill of self-renunciation. Here many are called and few are chosen. For every one that actually crosses over into the Promised Land, there are many who stand for a while and look longingly across the river, and then turn sadly back to the comparative safety of the sandy wastes of the old life.

The Holy Spirit will expect obedience to the written Word. We would like to be able to be filled with the Spirit, or full of the Spirit, and then more or less do as we please. But the Holy Spirit who inspired the Scriptures will expect obedience to the Scriptures. And if we do not obey the Scriptures, we will quench Him. He will have obedience and people do not want to obey the Lord.

"We are his witnesses of these things and so is also the Holy Ghost whom God hath given to them that obey him." There must be obedience there. Spirit of God will not give a disobedient child His blessing. He will not fill a disobedient child with the Holy Spirit. There must be obedience there. Obedience to the word, obedience to the Spirit, obedience to the risen Lord. You must be an obedient Christian. He gives His Holy Spirit to them that obey Him.

18. That Which is Flesh is Sin

Dead in Christ

The Scriptures say that every Christian believer may consider himself to have died in Christ. Give yourselves over for a time to the study of chapters 5 through 8 in the book of Romans. You will see for yourself that this is the doctrine of the Bible: When Christ became humanity, He made it possible for us to get up into deity—not to become deity but to be united with deity.

God counts Christ's death to be my death and He counts the sacrifice Christ laid down to be mine.

I repeat: *"For the love of Christ constraineth us; because we thus judge, that if one died for all, then were all dead ... that they which live should not henceforth live unto themselves."* (2 Corinthians 5:14-15)

No man has any right to sin again now—the voice of Jesus' blood is eloquent now, one of the most eloquent sounds in the human mind.

Wherever you find Christ's church, wherever her songs are raised, wherever the prayers of her saints rise we hear the voice of Jesus' blood pleading eloquently, and witnessing that "in the blood of Christ the sins of the world died" (see 1 John 2:2).

Oh, if men and women will only believe it!

When will we realize and confess that every sin is now a moral incongruity? As believers, we are supposed to have died with Jesus Christ our Lord. When we were joined to Him in the new birth we were joined to His death. When we were joined to His rising again, it should have been plain to us that sin is now a moral incongruity in the life of a Christian.

The sinner sins because he is out there in the world—and he has never died. He is waiting to die, and he will die once, and later he will die the second death.

But a Christian dies *with* Christ and dies *in* Christ and dies *along with* Christ, so that when he lays his body down at last, the Bible says he will not see death.

God will cover the eyes of all Christians when the time comes—they never see death. The Christian stops breathing and there is a burial but he does not see death—for he already died in Christ when Christ died, and he arose with Christ when Christ arose.

That is why sin is a moral incongruity in the life and deportment of the Christian believer. It is a doctrine and theology completely unknown to those whose Christianity is like a button or flower stuck on the lapel—completely external.

I believe the gospel of Jesus Christ saved me completely—therefore He asks me for total commitment. He expects me to be a disciple totally dedicated.

Joined to Jesus Christ, how can we be other than what He is? What He does, we do. Where He leads, we go. This is genuine Christianity!

Sin is now an outrage against holy blood. To sin now is to crucify the Son of God afresh. To sin now is to belittle the blood of atonement. For a Christian to sin now is to insult the holy life laid down. I cannot believe that any Christian wants to sin.

All offenses against God will either be forgiven or avenged—we can take our choice. All offenses against God, against ourselves, against humanity, against human life—all offenses will be either forgiven or avenged. There are two voices—one pleading for vengeance, the other pleading for mercy.

What a terrible thing for men and women to get old and have no prospect, no gracious promise for the long eternity before them.

But how beautiful to come up like a ripe shock of corn and know that the Father's house is open, the doors are wide open and the Father waits to receive His children one after another!

Some years ago, one of our national Christian brothers from the land of Thailand gave his testimony in my hearing. He told what it had meant in his life and for his future when the missionaries came with the good news of the gospel of Christ.

He described the godly life of one of the early missionaries and then said, "He is in the Father's house now."

He told of one of the missionary women and the love of Christ she had displayed and then said, "She is in the Father's house now."

What a vision for a humble Christian who only a generation before had been a pagan, worshiping idols and spirits—and now because of grace and mercy he talks about the Father's house as though it were just a step away, across the street.

This is the gospel of Christ—the kind of Christianity I believe in. What joy to discover that God is not mad at us and that we are His children—because Jesus died for us, because the blood of Jesus *"speaketh better things than that of Abel."* (Hebrews 12:24)

What a blessing to find out that the mercy of God speaks louder than the voice of justice. What a hope that makes it possible for the Lord's people to lie down quietly when the time comes and whisper, "Father, I am coming home!"

Oh, we ought to make more of the blood of the Lamb, because it is by the blood that we are saved; by the blood atonement is made.

You know I encourage you to sing some of the old camp meeting songs with plain theology and clear message. This is one of those:

> *The cross, the cross, the bloodstained cross,*
>
> *The hallowed cross I see;*
>
> *Reminding me of precious blood*
>
> *That once was shed for me.*

A thousand, thousand fountains spring

Up from the throne of God;

But none to me such blessings bring

As Jesus' precious blood.

That priceless blood my ransom paid

When I in bondage stood;

On Jesus all my sins were laid,

He saved me with His blood.

By faith that blood now sweeps away

My sins, as like a flood;

Nor lets one guilty blemish stay;

All praise to Jesus' blood!

This wondrous theme will best employ

My heart before my God;

And make all heaven resound with joy

For Jesus' cleansing blood.

The blood of Jesus Christ continues to plead eloquently. At the right hand of God the Father, I do not believe that Jesus, our great high priest, has to talk and talk. I am sure His intercession for us lies in His two wounded hands.

When children of God violate the covenant, God hears the voice of the wounded Son of God and forgives. But is that reason for us to be careless? Never! Never while the world stands!

We Christians ought to be the cleanest, purest, most righteous, holiest people in all the world—for the blood of Jesus Christ can sweep away our sins "as like a flood; nor lets one guilty blemish stay; all praise to Jesus' blood!"

Give Up to Obtain

Contrary to what professing Christians like to think, many of God's people are not willing to walk in perfect agreement with Him. This may explain why so many believers do not have the power of the Spirit, the peace of the Spirit, and many of the other qualities, gifts, and benefits that the Spirit of God brings.

The question is: Are we willing to walk with Him in love and obedience?

The answer is that we cannot walk with Him unless we are agreed; and if we are not agreed, we will not walk with Him in harmony and fruitfulness and blessing.

Many people in the churches who profess that they have an interest in the subject, "How to cultivate the Spirit's companionship," are not really willing to give up all to obtain all. They are not willing to turn completely toward God and walk with Him.

You may remember that John Bunyan, in his great allegorical writings, often mentioned Mr. Facing Bothways. We ought to know as well as he did that there are a great many Christians who try to accomplish the difficult task of facing in both directions at the same time. They do want Christ, but they also want some of the world. They allow the Lord to disturb their way, but they also disturb the Lord's way, and there is no use talking about being filled with the Spirit and walking in the Spirit unless we are willing to give up all to obtain all!

Now, this old question in the text, "Can two walk together except they be agreed?" is a rhetorical question, equivalent to a positive declaration that two *cannot* walk together except they be agreed, and the affirmation that if the two walk together, they must in some sense be one.

These two, in order to walk together, must agree that they want to walk together, and they must agree that it is to their advantage to have this companionship together. I think you will see that it all adds up to this: For two to walk together voluntarily, they must in some sense be one. They must be unified on the important issues of their walk and companionship and direction if they are going to be committed to traveling together.

Walk In Righteousness

Now, I have heard that a Christian brother has said, "Tozer doesn't distinguish between discipleship and salvation. You *can* be a Christian without being a disciple."

Just let me ask: Who said that you can be a Christian without being a disciple? I don't think you can be a Christian without being a disciple.

The idea that I can come to the Lord and by grace have all of my sins forgiven, have my name written in heaven, have the carpenter go to work on a mansion in my Father's house, and at the same time raise hell on my way to heaven, is impossible and unscriptural. It cannot be found in the Bible.

We are never saved by our good works, but we are not saved apart from good works. Out of our saving faith in Jesus Christ, there springs immediately goodness and righteousness. Spring is not brought by flowers, but you cannot have spring without flowers. It isn't my righteousness that saves, but the salvation I have received brings righteousness.

I think we must face up to this now—that we must walk in righteousness if we are going on to know the Lord. The man who is not ready to live right is not saved, and he will not be saved, and he will be deceived in that great day. The grace of God that bringeth salvation teaches the heart that we should deny ungodliness and worldly lusts and live soberly and righteously and godly in this present world.

There you have the three dimensions of life: soberly—that is me; righteously—that is my fellow man; and godly—that is God. We ought not to make the mistake of thinking that we can be spiritual and not be good.

I cannot believe that a man is on the road to heaven when he is habitually performing the kind of deeds that would logically indicate that he ought to be on his way to hell. How can the two walk together except they be agreed? He is the Holy Spirit, and if I walk an unholy way, how can I be in fellowship with Him?

Break with the World

The Christian is called to separation from the world, but we must be sure we know what we mean (or more important, what God means) by the *world*. We are likely to make it mean something external only and thus miss its real meaning. The theater, cards, liquor, gambling—these are not the world. They are merely an external manifestation of the world.

Our warfare is not against merely an external manifestation of the world. Our warfare is not against mere worldly ways, but against the *spirit* of the world. For man, whether he is saved or lost, is essentially spirit. The world, in the New Testament meaning of the word, is simply unregenerate human nature wherever it is found, whether in a tavern or in a church.

Whatever springs out of, is built upon, or receives support from fallen human nature, is the world—regardless of whether it is morally base or morally respectable.

The ancient Pharisees, in spite of their zealous devotion to religion, were of the very essence of the world. The spiritual principles upon which they built their system were drawn not from above but from below. They employed against Jesus the tactics of men.

They bribed men to tell lies in defense of truth. To defend God, they acted like devils. To support the Bible, they defied the teachings of the Bible. They scuttled religion to save religion. They gave rein to blind hate in the name of the religion of love.

There we see the world in all of its grim defiance of God. So fierce was this spirit that it never rested till it had put to death the Son of

God Himself. The spirit of the Pharisees was actively and maliciously hostile to the Spirit of Jesus as each was a kind of distillation of the two worlds from whence they came.

Those present-day teachers who place the Sermon on the Mount in some other dispensation than this and so release the Church from its teachings little realize the evil they do.

For the Sermon on the Mount gives in brief the characteristics of the kingdom of renewed men. The blessed poor who mourn for their sins and thirst after righteousness are true sons of the kingdom. In meekness they show mercy to their enemies; with guileless candor they gaze upon God; surrounded by persecutors they bless and curse not. In modesty they hide their good deeds.

They go out of their way to agree with their adversaries and forgive those who sin against them. They serve God in secret in the depth of their hearts and wait with patience for His open reward. They freely surrender their earthly goods rather than use violence to protect them. They lay up treasures in heaven. They avoid praise and wait for the day of final reckoning to learn who is greatest in the kingdom of heaven.

If this is a fairly accurate view of things, what can we say then when Christian men vie with one another for place and position? What can we answer when we see them hungrily seeking for praise and honor? How can we excuse the passion for publicity which is so glaringly evident among Christian leaders?

What about political ambition in Church circles? What about the fevered palm that is stretched out for more and bigger "love offerings"? What about the shameless egotism among Christians? How can we explain the gross man-worship that habitually blows up one and another popular leader to the size of colossus? What about the obsequious hand-kissing of moneyed men by those purporting to be sound preachers of the gospel?

There is only one answer to these questions. It is simply that in these manifestations we see the world, and nothing but the world. No passionate profession of love for "souls" can change evil into good. These are the very sins that crucified Jesus.

It is also true that the grosser manifestations of fallen human nature are part of the kingdom of this world. Organized amusements with their emphasis upon shallow pleasure, the great empires built upon vicious and unnatural habits, unrestrained abuse of normal appetites, the artificial world called "high society"—these are all of the world. They are all part of that which is flesh, which builds upon flesh and must perish with the flesh.

And from these things the Christian must flee. All these he must put behind him and in them he must have no part. Against them he must stand quietly but firmly without compromise and without fear.

So, whether the world presents itself in its uglier aspects or in its subtler and more refined forms, we must recognize it for what it is and repudiate it bluntly. We must do this if we would walk with God in our generation as Enoch did in his. A clean break with the world is imperative.

Ye adulterers and adulteresses, know ye not that the friendship of the world is enmity with God? whosoever therefore will be a friend of the world is the enemy of God. (James 4:4)

Love not the world, neither the things that are in the world. If any man love the world, the love of the Father is not in him. For all that is in the world, the lust of the flesh, and the lust of the eyes, and the pride of life, is not of the Father, but is of the world. (1 John 2:15-16)

These words of God are not before us for our consideration; they are there for our obedience and we have no right to claim the title of Christian unless we follow them.

For myself, I fear any kind of religious stir among Christians that does not lead to repentance and result in a sharp separation of the believer from the world. I am suspicious of any organized revival effort that is forced to play down the hard terms of the kingdom. No matter how attractive the movement may appear, if it is not founded in righteousness and nurtured in humility, it is not of God. If it exploits the flesh, it is a religious fraud and should not have the support of any God-fearing Christian. Only that is of God which honors the Spirit and prospers at the expense of the human ego.

"That, according as it is written, He that glorieth, let him glory in the Lord." (1 Corinthians 1:31)

19.Count the Cost

No Rivalling Interests

A few things, fortunately only a few, are matters of life and death, such as a compass for a sea voyage or a guide for a journey across the desert. To ignore these vital things is not to gamble or take a chance; it is to commit suicide. Here it is either be right or be dead.

Our relation to Christ is such a matter of life or death, and on a much higher plane. The Bible-instructed man knows that Jesus Christ came into the world to save sinners, and that men are saved by Christ alone altogether apart from any works of merit.

That much is true and is known, but obviously the death and resurrection of Christ do not automatically save everyone. How does the individual man come into saving relation to Christ? We know that some *do*, but that others do *not* is evident.

How is the gulf bridged between redemption objectively provided and salvation subjectively received? How does that which Christ did for me become operative within me?

To the question "What must I do to be saved?" we must learn the correct answer. To fail here is not to gamble with our souls; it is to guarantee eternal banishment from the face of God. Here we must be right or be finally lost.

To this anxious question evangelical Christians provide three answers, "Believe on the Lord Jesus Christ," "Receive Christ as your personal Savior," and "Accept Christ." Two of the answers are drawn almost verbatim from Scripture (Acts 16:31, John 1:12), while the third is a kind of paraphrase meant to sum up the other two. They are therefore not three but one.

Being spiritually lazy, we naturally tend to gravitate toward the easiest way of settling our religious questions for ourselves and others. Hence the formula "Accept Christ" has become a panacea of universal application, and I believe it has been fatal to many.

An occasional serious-minded penitent may undoubtedly find in it all the instruction he needs to bring him into living contact with Christ. But I fear that too many seekers use it as a shortcut to the Promised Land, only to find that it has led them instead to *"a land of darkness, as darkness itself; and of the shadow of death, without any order, and where the light is as darkness."* (Job 10:22)

The trouble is that the whole "Accept Christ" attitude is likely to be wrong. It shows Christ applying to us, rather than us to Him. It makes Him stand, hat in hand, awaiting our verdict on Him, instead of our kneeling with troubled hearts awaiting His verdict on us. It may even permit us to accept Christ by an impulse of mind or emotions, painlessly, at no loss to our ego and no inconvenience to our usual way of life.

For this ineffectual manner of dealing with a vital matter we might imagine some parallels; as if, for instance, Israel in Egypt had "accepted" the blood of the Passover but continued to live in bondage, or the prodigal son had "accepted" his father's forgiveness and stayed on among the swine in the far country. Is it not plain that if accepting Christ is to mean anything there must be moral action that accords with it?

Allowing the expression "Accept Christ" to stand as an honest effort to say in short what could not be so well said any other way, let us see what we mean or should mean when we use it.

To accept Christ is to form an attachment to the Person of our Lord Jesus altogether unique in human experience. The attachment is intellectual, volitional and emotional. The believer is intellectually convinced that Jesus is both Lord and Christ; he has set his will to follow Him at any cost and soon his heart is enjoying the exquisite sweetness of His fellowship.

This attachment is all-inclusive in that it joyfully accepts Christ for all that He is. There is no craven division of offices whereby we may acknowledge His Saviorhood today and withhold decision on His Lordship till tomorrow. The true believer owns Christ as his All in All without reservation. He also includes all of himself, leaving no part of his being unaffected by the revolutionary transaction.

Further, his attachment to Christ is all-exclusive. The Lord becomes to him not one of several rival interests, but the one exclusive attraction forever. He orbits around Christ as the earth around the sun, held in thrall by the magnetism of His love, drawing all his life and light and warmth from Him. In this happy state he is given other interests, it is true, but these are all determined by his relation to his Lord.

That we accept Christ in this all-inclusive, all-exclusive way is a divine imperative. Here faith makes its leap into God through the Person and work of Christ, but it never divides the work from the Person. It never tries to believe on the blood apart from Christ Himself, or the cross or the "finished work." It believes on the Lord Jesus Christ, the whole Christ without modification or reservation, and thus it receives and enjoys all that He did in His work of redemption, all that He is now doing in heaven for His own and all that He does in and through them.

To accept Christ is to know the meaning of the words *"as he is, so are we in this world."* (1 John 4:17)

We accept His friends as our friends, His enemies as our enemies, His ways as our ways, His rejection as our rejection, His cross as our cross, His life as our life and His future as our future.

If this is what we mean when we advise the seeker to accept Christ, we had better explain it to him. He may get into deep spiritual trouble unless we do.

An Enemy of Satan

As we move farther on and mount higher up in the Christian life, we may expect to encounter greater difficulties in the way and meet increased hostility from the enemy of our souls. Though this is seldom presented to Christians as a fact of life, it is a very solid fact indeed as every experienced Christian knows, and one we shall learn how to handle, or stumble over to our own undoing.

Satan hates the true Christian for several reasons. One is that God loves him, and whatever is loved by God is sure to be hated by the devil. Another is that the Christian, being a child of God, bears a family resemblance to the Father and to the household of faith. Satan's ancient jealousy has not abated nor his hatred for God diminished in the slightest. Whatever reminds him of God is without other reason the object of his malignant hate.

A third reason is that a true Christian is a former slave who has escaped from the galley, and Satan cannot forgive him for this affront. A fourth reason is that a praying Christian is a constant threat to the stability of Satan's government. The Christian is a holy rebel, loose in the world and with access to the throne of God. Satan never knows from what direction the danger will come.

Who knows when another Elijah will arise, or another Daniel? Or a Luther or a Booth? Who knows when an Edwards or a Finney may go in and liberate a whole town or countryside by the preaching of the Word and prayer? Such a danger is too great to tolerate, so Satan gets to the new convert as early as possible to prevent his becoming too formidable a foe.

The new believer thus becomes at once a principal target for the fiery darts of the devil. Satan knows that the best way to be rid of a soldier is to destroy him before he becomes a man. The young Moses must not be allowed to grow into a liberator to set a nation free. The Baby Jesus dare not be permitted to become a man to die for the sins of the world. The new Christian must be destroyed early, or at least he must have his growth stunted so that he will be no real problem later.

Now I do not think that Satan much cares to destroy us Christians physically. The soldier dead in battle who died performing some deed of heroism is not a great loss to the army but may rather be an object of pride to his country. On the other hand, the soldier who cannot or will not fight but runs away at the sound of the first enemy gun is a shame to his family and a disgrace to his nation.

So a Christian who dies in the faith represents no irreparable loss to the forces of righteousness on earth and certainly no victory for the devil. But when whole regiments of professed believers are too timid to fight and too smug to be ashamed, surely it must bring an astringent smile to the face of the enemy. And it should bring a blush to the cheeks of the whole Church of Christ.

The devil's master strategy for us Christians then is not to kill us physically (though there may be some special situations where physical death fits into his plan better), but to destroy our power to wage spiritual warfare.

And how well he has succeeded. The average Christian these days is a harmless enough thing, God knows. He is a child wearing with considerable self-consciousness the harness of the warrior; he is a sick eaglet that can never mount up with wings; he is a spent pilgrim who has given up the journey and sits with a waxy smile trying to get what pleasure he can from sniffing the wilted flowers he has plucked by the way.

Such as these have been reached. Satan has gotten to them early. By means of false teaching, or inadequate teaching, or the huge discouragement that comes from the example of a decadent church, he has succeeded in weakening their resolution, neutralizing their convictions and taming their original urge to do exploits. Now they are little more than statistics that contribute financially to the upkeep of the religious institution. And how many a pastor is content to act as a patient, smiling curator of a church full (or a quarter full) of such blessed spiritual museum pieces.

If Satan opposes the new convert, he opposes still more bitterly the Christian who is pressing on toward a higher life in Christ. The Spirit-filled life is not, as many suppose, a life of peace and quiet pleasure. It is likely to be something quite the opposite.

Viewed one way it is a pilgrimage through a robber-infested forest; viewed another, it is a grim warfare with the devil. Always there is struggle, and sometimes there is a pitched battle with our own nature where the lines are so confused that it is all but impossible to locate the enemy or to tell which impulse is of the Spirit and which of the flesh.

To accept the call of Christ changes the returning sinner indeed, but it does not change the world. The wind still blows toward hell, and the man who is walking in the opposite direction will have the wind in his face. And we had better take this into account when we ponder on spiritual things. If the unsearchable riches of Christ are not worth suffering for, then we should know it now and cease to play at religion.

Nothing that man has discovered about himself or God has revealed

any shortcut to pure spirituality. It is still free, but tremendously costly.

There is complete victory for us if we will but take the way of the
triumphant Christ, but that is not what we are considering now. My
point here is that if we want to escape the struggle we have but to
draw back and accept the currently accepted low-keyed Christian
life as the normal one. That is all Satan wants. That will ground our
power, stunt our growth and render us harmless to the kingdom of
darkness.

Compromise will take the pressure off. Satan will not bother a man
who has quit fighting. But the cost of quitting will be a life of peace-
ful stagnation. We sons of eternity just cannot afford such a thing.

20.Accept Disciplining

For he was looking forward to the city with foundations,

whose architect and builder is God.

HEBREWS 11:10

Preparing For Heaven

I have found there is an entirely new way to shock complacent Christians in our churches today. These Christians go into shock when I say that it is an error to assume that being saved is to be automatically ready for heaven. Very few people in our churches are willing to consider what the Bible actually teaches about discipline and chastening in preparing us for our heavenly home. The writer of the letter to the Hebrews gave definite instruction to those who were children of God through faith in our Lord Jesus Christ:

If ye endure chastening, God dealeth with you as with sons; for what son is he whom the father chasteneth not? But if ye be without chastisement, whereof all are partakers, then are ye bastards, and not sons.... He [chastens us] for our profit, that we might be partakers of his holiness.... Follow peace with all men, and holiness, without which no man shall see the Lord. (Heb. 12:7–14)

Now, I know I will have to explain what I mean about our daily Christian lives being in preparation for an eternity in the heavenly realms. First, let us see if we are in agreement about the most important proclamation we can make concerning faith.

There is no doubt about it. First in importance concerning faith is the good news—the truth that every man and woman in our lost world may have God's gifts of forgiveness and eternal life through believing faith in Jesus Christ as Savior and Lord.

It is not possible to overstate the importance of this basic truth in the Christian gospel. It has been proclaimed often. Paul gave this stark, simple instruction concerning salvation to the jailer at Philippi: *"Believe on the Lord Jesus Christ, and thou shalt be saved, and thy house."* (Acts 16:31)

As Christian believers (I am assuming you are a believer), you and I know how we have been changed and regenerated and assured of eternal life by faith in Jesus Christ and His atoning death. On the other hand, where this good news of salvation by faith is not known, religion becomes an actual bondage. If Christianity is known only as a religious institution, it may well become merely a legalistic system of religion, and the hope of eternal life becomes a delusion.

I have said this much about the reality and assurance of our salvation through Jesus Christ to counter the shock you may feel when I add that God wants to fully prepare you in your daily Christian life so that you will be ready indeed for heaven. Perhaps it is a good thing for you if you are shocked. It is my observation that many Christians are so cosmopolitan, so worldly wise, so self-assured that they are past being shocked by anything!

Probably your first question as you come out of shock will be, "Have you forgotten the dying thief? Did not our Lord tell him his faith had made him ready for paradise?"

Let me share something with you. No one could love the Christian gospel and witness it to others without an understanding that the God of all grace has surely made a necessary provision for those who may trust Jesus in the final hours of life. We admit our humanness. We do not have God's wisdom and discernment. Only God is all-knowing and all-powerful. He is full of grace and truth. We can trust Him to be faithful and right in all of His dealings with us.

Remember that most believers have been found of the Lord and re-ceived His love and grace at an earlier time in their lives. Many testi-fy to faith extending back to their childhood. Thus, they have been in God's household for a long time, and He has been trying to do some-thing special within their beings day after day, year after year. His purpose has been to bring many sons—and daughters, too—to glory.

Now, if we are truly sons and daughters by faith, we will respond to the wise discipline and the necessary rebukes aimed at bringing us to the full measure of spiritual stature. God's motives are loving. Our heavenly Father disciplines us for our own good, *"that we might be partakers of his holiness."* (Heb. 12:10)

I have known people who seemed to be terrified by God's loving desire that we should reflect His own holiness and goodness. As God's faithful children, we should be attracted to holiness, for holiness is God-likeness—likeness to God!

God encourages every Christian believer to follow after holiness. Holiness is to be our constant ambition—not as holy as God is holy, but holy because God is holy. We know who we are and God knows who He is. He does not ask us to be God, and He does not ask us to produce the holiness that only He Himself knows. Only God is holy absolutely; all other beings can be holy only in relative degrees.

The angels in heaven do not possess God's holiness. They are created beings and they are contented to reflect the glory of God. That is their holiness.

Holiness is not terrifying. Actually, it is amazing and wonderful that God should promise us the privilege of sharing in His nature. It is impossible for any person to be as holy as God is holy. It is encouraging that God *"knoweth our frame."* (Ps. 103:14) He remembers we were made of dust. So He tells us what is in His being as He thinks of us: "Be holy because I am your God and I am holy! It is My desire that you grow in grace and in the knowledge of Me. I want you to be more like Jesus, My eternal Son, every day you live!"

Our Lord endeavors to prepare us for our eternal fellowship with the saints, the martyrs, the heroes of the faith who suffered through fire and flood and blood and tears when they were God's pilgrims on this earth. Do not try to short-circuit God's plans for your discipleship and spiritual maturing here. If you and I were already prepared for heaven in that moment of our conversion, God would have taken us there instantly!

God's Incomprehensible Holiness

As believers and disciples, we are satisfied to know that the mysterious quality of God's holy person sets Him apart from all others and all else throughout His entire universe. God exists in Himself. His holy nature is such that we cannot comprehend Him with our minds.

God's holy nature is unique. He is of a substance not shared by any other being. Hence, God can be known only as He reveals Himself. There is absolutely no other way for us to know Him.

In Old Testament times, whenever this utterly holy God revealed Himself in some way to mankind, terror and amazement were the reaction. People saw themselves as guilty and unclean by contrast.

Early in the Revelation, the final book of the Bible, the apostle John describes the overwhelming nature of his encounter with the Lord of glory. He says, *"And when I saw him, I fell at his feet as dead."* (Rev. 1:17) John was a man, a person born into a sinful world. But he was a believer and an apostle. At the time, he was in exile *"for the word of God, and for the testimony of Jesus Christ."* (1:9) But when the risen, glorified Lord Jesus appeared to him on Patmos, John sank down in abject humility and fear.

Jesus at once reassured him, stooping to place a nail-pierced hand on the prostrate apostle. *"Fear not,"* Jesus said to John. *"I am the first and the last: I am he that liveth, and was dead; and, behold, I am alive for evermore, Amen; and have the keys of hell and of death."* (1:17–18) Then Jesus proceeded to give His apostle a writing assignment: *"Write the things which thou hast seen, and the things which are, and the things which shall be hereafter."* (1:19)

I notice particularly that the Lord did not condemn John. He knew that John's weakness was the reaction to revealed divine strength. He knew that John's sense of unworthiness was the instant reaction to absolute holiness. Along with John, every redeemed human being needs the humility of spirit that can only be brought about by the manifest presence of God.

This mysterious yet gracious Presence is the air of life eternal. It is the music of existence, the poetry of the Christian life. It is the beauty and wonder of being one of Christ's own—a sinner born again, regenerated, created anew to bring glory to God. To know this Presence is the most desirable state imaginable for anyone. To live surrounded by this sense of God is not only beautiful and desirable, but it is also imperative!

Know that our living Lord is unspeakably pure. He is sinless, spotless, immaculate, stainless. In His person is an absolute fullness of purity that our words can never express. This fact alone changes our entire human and moral situation and outlook. We can always be sure of the most important of all positives: God is God and God is right. He is in control. Because He is God He will never change!

I repeat: God is right—always. That statement is the basis of all we are thinking about God.

When the eternal God Himself invites us to prepare ourselves to be with Him throughout the future ages, we can only bow in delight and gratitude, murmuring, "Oh, Lord, may Your will be done in this poor, unworthy life!"

I can only hope that you are wise enough, desirous enough and spiritual enough to face up to the truth that every day is another day of spiritual preparation, another day of testing and discipline with our heavenly destination in mind. For as I hope you have already seen, full qualification for eternity is not instant or automatic or painless.

I hope, too, that you may begin to understand in this context why our evangelical churches are in such a mess. It has become popular to preach a painless Christianity and automatic saintliness. It has become a part of our "instant" culture. "Just pour a little water on it, stir mildly, pick up a gospel tract, and you are on your Christian way."

Lo, we are told, this is Bible Christianity. *It is nothing of the sort!* To depend upon that kind of a formula is to experience only the outer fringe, the edge of what Christianity really is. We must be committed to all that it means to believe in the Lord Jesus Christ. There must be a new birth from above; otherwise we are in religious bondage and legalism and delusion—or worse! But when the wonder of regeneration has taken place in our lives, then comes the lifetime of preparation with the guidance of the Holy Spirit.

God has told us that heaven and the glories of the heavenly kingdom are more than humans can ever dream or imagine. It will be neither an exhibition of the commonplace nor a democracy for the spiritually mediocre.

God's Plan for Our Spiritual Maturity

Why should we try to be detractors of God's gracious and rewarding plan of discipleship? God has high plans for all of His redeemed ones. It is inherent in His infinite being that His motives are love and goodness. His plans for us come out of His eternal and creative wisdom and power. Beyond that is His knowledge and regard for the astonishing potential that lies resident in human nature, long asleep in sin but awakened by the Holy Spirit in regeneration.

Yes, God is preparing us by making us disciples of Christ. A disciple is one who is in training. Being a disciple of Christ brings us to the day-by-day realities of such terms as discipline, rebuke, correction, hardship. Those are not pleasant words. To be admonished and instructed, to be punished and reproved, to be trained and corrected—no one chooses these things because they are neither pleasant nor entertaining. But they are in God's plan for our spiritual maturity.

In times of testing and hardship, I have heard Christians cry in their discouragement, "How can I believe that God loves me?" The fact is, God loves us to such a degree that He will use every necessary means to mature us until we reach "unity of the faith" and attain "unto the measure of the stature of the fulness of Christ" (Eph. 4:13).

A critic may cringe and charge that God is breaking our spirits, that we will be worth nothing as a result, that we will wear only a sad, hang-dog look for eternity. Oh, no! That is not true. What God plans is to bring us into accord with the wisdom and power and holiness that flow eternally from His throne.

God's loving motive is to bring us into total harmony with Himself so that moral power and holy usefulness become ours in this world and in the world to come.

This has been a message from my heart about down-to-earth preparation that will result in readiness for heaven's joys. Let me therefore conclude with a simple, down-to-earth illustration—the example of a newborn baby brought suddenly into the confusion of our noisy world.

Is the little fellow "ready" for this world in which he must live? When the time of his birth neared, the doctor told the parents-to-be, "The baby is ready!" So, as the baby was born, it could have been said in the biological sense that he was "ready."

But what do you really think? You must know that the baby is not really ready at all! From the first little whack he gets to make him cry and get his breath right on for the next eighteen or twenty years, that baby and child and young man will need to learn much about his environment. He will need to mature day by day.

In the broader social and human sense, he is not ready for this world until years have passed and he has completed his formal education. So it is with the Christian believer who has confessed his or her faith in Jesus Christ. Oh, yes, he or she is forgiven and "saved." But is he, is she automatically prepared for heaven and all of the eternal glories above?

To say yes is to be ridiculous. You might as well say that you can pick up a newborn baby, prop him up in the chair of the nation's President or Prime Minister and whisper in his ear that he is ready to govern.

My mind returns frequently to some of the old Christian saints who often prayed in their faith, "O God, we know this world is only a dressing room for the heaven to come!" They were very close to the truth in their vision of what God has planned for His children.

In summary: Down here the orchestra merely rehearses; over there we will give the concert. Here, we ready our garments of righteousness; over there we will wear them at the wedding of the Lamb.

21.True Fulfillment

God Knows What Is Fulfilling

God being God of infinite goodness must by the necessity of His nature will for each of His creatures the fullest measure of happiness consistent with its capacities and with the happiness of all other creatures.

Furthermore, being omniscient and omnipotent, God has the wisdom and power to achieve whatever He wills. The redemption which He provided for us through the incarnation, death and resurrection of His only Son guarantees eternal blessedness to all who through faith become beneficiaries of that redemption.

This the Church teaches her children to believe, and her teaching is more than hopeful thinking. It is founded upon the fullest and plainest revelations of the Old and New Testaments. That it accords with the most sacred yearnings of the human heart does not in any manner weaken it, but serves rather to confirm the truth of it, since the One who made the heart might be expected also to make provision for the fulfillment of its deepest longings.

Our inner fulfilment lies in loving obedience to the commandments of Christ and the inspired admonitions of His apostles. The need to know God Himself is the ultimate goal of all Christian doctrine.

"It is God which worketh in you." He needs no one, but when faith is present He works through anyone. Two statements are in this sentence and a healthy spiritual life requires that we accept both.

Between Two Worlds

In the Kingdom of God, the surest way to lose something is to try to protect it, and the best way to keep it is to let it go.

The law of keeping by surrendering and losing by defending is revealed by our Lord in His celebrated but little understood declaration: "*If any man will come after me, let him deny himself, and take up his cross, and follow me.*" (Matt. 16:24)

Here is seen the glaring disparity between the ways of God and the ways of men. When the world takes its hands off a prized possession someone grabs it and disappears. The world must conserve by defending.

So, men hoard their hearts treasures, lock up their possessions, protect their good name with libel laws, hedge themselves about with protective devices of every sort and guard their shores with powerful armed forces. This is all according to Adam's philosophy which springs from his fallen nature and is confirmed by thousands of years of practical experience. To challenge it is to invite the scow of mankind; and yet our Lord did challenge it.

To be specific, Christ did not condemn the world for defending its own; He turned from the fallen world and spoke about another world altogether, a world where Adam's philosophy is invalid and where his techniques are inoperative. He spoke of the kingdom of God whose laws are exactly opposite to those of the kingdom of man.

Long before Christ laid down the spiritual principles that should govern the new kingdom God had said by the mouth of His prophet, "*My thoughts are not your thoughts, neither are your ways my ways,*" (Isa. 53:8)

Christ said elsewhere, "*That which is highly esteemed among men is abomination in the sight of God.*" (Luke 16:15)

Between spiritual laws and the laws of human society there is a great gulf. In His wisdom God moves on the high road according to His eternal purposes; man on the low road moves along as best he can, improvising and muddling through according to no certain plan, hoping that things will come out all right and almost always seeing his hopes disappointed.

The true Christian is a child of two worlds. He lives among fallen men, receives all of his earlier concepts from them and develops a fallen view of life along with everyone from Adam on. When he is regenerated and inducted into the new creation he is called to live according to the laws and principles that underlie the new kingdom, but all his training and his thinking have been according to the old. So he may, unless he is very wise and prayerful, find himself trying to live a heavenly life after an earthly pattern. This is what Paul called "carnal" living. The issues of the new Christian life are influenced by the automatic responses of the old life and confusion results.

Against this background it is easy to understand why so many Christians instinctively cling to their treasures, defend their possessions and fight for their reputation. They are reacting after the old pattern which they had followed so naturally and so long.

It takes real faith to begin to live the life of heaven while still upon the earth, for this requires that we rise above the law of moral gravitation and bring to our everyday living the high wisdom of God. And since this wisdom is contrary to that of the world, conflict is bound to result. This, however, is a small price to pay for the inestimable privilege of following Christ.

It is vitally important that we move up into the Spirit and cease to defend ourselves. I have never met a victorious Christian who was on the defensive, but I have met I cannot tell how many jumpy, skittish and thoroughly unhappy Christians who were burning up their energies in a vain endeavor to protect themselves. These poor, dejected souls imagine that someone is forever trying, as they say, to "put something over" on them. The result is worry, resentfulness and a kind of low-pressure hostility toward everyone they may have reason to believe is after something they possess.

My earnest advice to all such nervous souls is to turn everything over to God and relax. A real Christian need not defend his possession nor his position. God will take care of both. Let go of your treasures and the Lord will keep them for you unto life eternal. Hang unto them and they will bring you nothing but trouble and misery to the end of your days.

It is better to throw our little all to the four winds than to get old and sour defending it. It is better to be cheated a few times than to develop a constant suspicion that someone is trying to cheat us. It is better to have the house burglarized than to spend the rest of our days and nights sitting with a rifle across our knees watching over it. Give it up, and keep it. Defend it, and lose it. That is a law of the kingdom and it applies to every regenerated soul.

We can afford to trust God; but we can't afford not to.

Fruits of Obedience

The Church of our day has soft-pedaled the doctrine of obedience, either neglecting it altogether or mentioning it only apologetically and without urgency. This results from a fundamental confusion of obedience with works in the minds of preacher and people. To escape the error of salvation by works we have fallen into the opposite error of salvation without obedience. In our eagerness to get rid of the legalistic doctrine of works we have thrown out the baby with the bath and gotten rid of obedience as well.

Look at the fruits of obedience as described in the New Testament.

The house of the obedient man is builded upon a rock (Matt. 7:24). He shall be loved by the Father and shall have the manifestation of the Father and the Son, who will come unto him and make their abode with him (John 14:21, 23). He shall abide in the love of Christ (John 15:10). By obedience to the doctrines of Christ he is set free from sin and made a servant of righteousness (Rom. 6:17, 18).

The Holy Spirit is given to him (Acts 5:32). He is delivered from self-deception and blessed in his deeds (James 1:22- 25). His faith is perfected (James 2:22). He is confirmed in his assurance toward God and given confidence in prayer, so that what he asks is given to him (1 John 3:18-22).

These are only a few among the many verses that may be cited from the New Testament. But more to the point than any number of proof texts is the fact that the whole drift of the New Testament is in that direction. One or two texts might be misunderstood, but there is no mistaking the whole tenor of Scripture.

What does all this add up to? What are its practical implications for us today? Just that the power of God is at our disposal, waiting for us to call it into action by meeting the conditions which are plainly laid down. God is ready to send down floods of blessing upon us as we begin to obey His plain instructions. We need no new doctrine, no new movement, no "key," no imported evangelist or expensive "course" to show us the way. It is before us as clear as a four-lane highway.

To any inquirer I would say, just do the next thing you know you should do to carry out the will of the Lord. If there is sin in your life, quit it instantly. Put away lying, gossiping, dishonesty, or whatever your sin may be. Forsake worldly pleasures, extravagance in spending, vanity in dress, in your car, in your home. Get right with any person you may have wronged. Forgive everyone who may have wronged you. Begin to use your money to help the poor and advance the cause of Christ. Take up the Cross and live sacrificially. Pray, attend the Lord's services. Witness for Christ, not only when it is convenient but when you know you should. Look to no cost and fear no consequences. Study the Bible to learn the will of God and then do His will as you understand it. Start now by doing the next thing, and then go on from there.

www.ingramcontent.com/pod-product-compliance
Lightning Source LLC
LaVergne TN
LVHW051540170726
843492LV00006B/1865